THE SPECTRUM OF

MUSIC

with Related Arts

Illustrated by
Tom Balchunas
James Barkley
Frank Bozzo
Anatoly Dverin
Bill Greer
Bob Schulenberg
Photos by
Alfred Fisher
Cover Design by Thomas Upshur

THE SPECTRUM OF

MUSIC

with Related Arts

A Macmillan/Schirmer program

Mary Val Marsh
Carroll Rinehart
Edith Savage

Macmillan Publishing Co., Inc.
New York

Collier Macmillan Publishers
London

ACKNOWLEDGMENTS

Grateful acknowledgment is given to the following authors and publishers:

Abingdon Press for "Remember September" from WINDS A'BLOWING by May Justus. Copyright © 1940 by May Justus, © 1961 by Abingdon Press. Used by permission.

Archon Books for "Washing Day" from FOLK SONGS OF OLD NEW ENGLAND by Linscott, second edition, 1962. Used by permission.

Bowmar Records, Inc. for "Chanukah Is Here" from HOLIDAY SONGS by Mills and Rinehart. Used by permission.

Bill Brohn for the music of "Changing" and "Baroquin' Rock," words by George Guilbault. Used by permission.

Byron-Douglas Publications for "Navy Hymn" by James D. Ployhar. Used by permission.

The Church of Jesus Christ of Latter-Day Saints for "Come, Come, Ye Saints" from LATTER-DAY SAINTS HYMNS by William Clayton. Used by permission of the Corporation of the President of the Church of Jesus Christ of Latter-Day Saints.

Cooperative Recreation Services, Inc. for "Haidschi, Bumbaidschi" from ANN ARBOR SINGS; "Chicka-Hanka" from LOOK AWAY; "Cuckoo," "Sourwood Mountain," "I'm Gonna Sing," "La Calle Ancha," and "The Winter Now Is Over" from SONGS TO KEEP; "The Singing School," "Shalom Chaverim" from 101 ROUNDS FOR SINGING; "Tiritomba," "Sing Your Way Home," and "Swinging Along" from SING A TUNE; "My Home's in Montana" from FUN AND FOLK SONGS; "Holla Hi," "Down in the Valley" from JOYFUL SINGING; "Hawaiian Surf" from ALOHA SAMPLER; and "Come and Dance" from HAPPY MEETING. Used by permission.

The Curtis Publishing Company for "Springtime Is a Green Time" by Rowena Bennett. Used by permission of The Curtis Publishing Company.

Hargail Music Company for "The Instruments" by Willie Geisler from HUMOR IN VOCAL MUSIC by Julius Hereford, 1927. Used by permission.

David Higham Associates, Ltd. for "Welcome to the New Year" from POEMS FOR CHILDREN by Eleanor Farjeon. Used by permission.

Jan-Lee Music for "Let There Be Peace on Earth" by Jill Jackson and Sy Miller. Copyright 1955. Used by permission.

The Instructor Publications, Inc. for "American Heritage," by Elsie Walush from INSTRUCTOR copyright © 1964. The Instructor Publications, Inc. Used by permission.

Jewish Educational Committee of New York for "Let Us Sing and Rejoice" ("N'ran'na") from THE NEW JEWISH SONG BOOK by Harry Coopersmith. Used by permission.

J.B. Lippincott Company for "Welcome to the New Year" from POEMS FOR CHILDREN by Eleanor Farjeon. Copyright © 1925, 1955 by Eleanor Farjeon. Used by permission of J.B. Lippincott.

Mele Loke Publishing Company for "Mahalo Nui" by Carol Roes and Lloyd Stone. Reprinted by permission of the Mele Loke Publishing Company.

Parts of this work were published in earlier editions of *The Spectrum of Music with Related Arts.*

Macmillan Publishing Co., Inc.
866 Third Avenue, New York, New York 10022
Collier Macmillan Canada, Inc.

Printed in the United States of America
ISBN 0-02-291940-6
9 8

AUTHORS

Mary Val Marsh has been a member of the Music Education faculty of San Diego State University and is well known as a workshop clinician. She has had extensive experience teaching and supervising classroom music at every level from kindergarten through graduate school and is the author of *Choruses and Carols, Here a Song, There a Song,* and *Explore and Discover Music.*

Carroll A. Rinehart has been Coordinator of Elementary music and a principal of an alternative open-education school in the Tucson, Arizona, Unified School District. He has served as a consultant and workshop clinician on the Manhattanville Music Curriculum Project. He is author of five choral collections.

Edith J. Savage, Professor of Music, San Diego State University, has taught and supervised classroom teachers of music at every level from kindergarten through graduate school. She is the co-author of *Teaching Children to Sing,* and co-author of *First Experience in Music,* a college text for elementary teachers.

CONSULTANTS

William Brohn, consultant in rock and popular music, is a conductor, performer, and arranger in New York City.

Venoris Cates, consultant in Afro-American music, is a music supervisor in the Chicago Public Schools and has had long experience teaching music in elementary schools.

Wayne Johnson, musicology consultant, is Chairman of the Department of Music, Georgetown College, Georgetown, Ky.

Walter E. Purdy, consultant in music education, is Coordinator of Music Education, University of Houston.

John Rouillard, consultant in American Indian music, is a member of a Sioux tribe. He is in charge of the program of Indian studies, San Diego State University.

Jose Villarino, consultant in Mexican-American music, is an Assistant Professor of Mexican-American studies, San Diego State University.

David L. Wilmot, general consultant on the Teacher's Annotated Edition, is a Professor of Music Education, University of Florida at Gainesville.

Contents

THE MEDIA OF MUSIC 1

LEARNING ABOUT VOICES 2
Expressing feelings through song 4
Your speaking voice 13
Your singing voice 18

EXPLORING PERCUSSION INSTRUMENTS 28
Create your own percussion music 30
Creating more percussion music 36

EXPLORING STRINGS 37
The harp 43

THE SYMPHONY ORCHESTRA 45
Knowing the score 52

EXPLORING MUSIC WITH TAPE RECORDERS 54
Composing with tape recorders 56

THE COMPONENTS OF MUSIC 61

RHYTHM IN MUSIC 62
Musical arithmetic 67
Rhythm patterns 68

RELATED ARTS
Works of Art
"Little Painting with Yellow," Wassily
  Kandinsky, 1
"The Hay Wain," John Constable, 6
"The Harvest," Vincent Van Gogh, 7
"Grey and Gold," John Rogers Cox, 15
"The Shrimp Girl," William Hogarth, 22
"Christ with the Sick Around Him,
  Receiving Little Children," Rembrandt, 25
"Sky Cathedral," Louise Nevelson, 31
"Fragments for the Gates to Times
  Square," Chryssa, 55
"The White Flower," Georgia O'Keeffe, 60
"Two Cats," Franz Marc, 66

"Rhythm of a Russian Dance," Theo van
  Doesburg, 71
"Jungle with a Lion," Henri Rousseau, 72
"Revolution of the Viaducts," Paul Klee, 75
"Cake Walk," Albert Meyers, 79
"Merz 83: Drawing F." Kurt Schwitters, 80
"Church Bells Ringing—Rainy Winter
  Night," Charles E. Burchfield, 91
"Singing Man," Ernst Barlach, 103
"Three-way Plug," Claus Oldenburg, 105
"Fog Horns," Arthur Dove, 108
"Carnival of Harlequin," Joan Miró, 118
"Figure for a Reliquary" (Congo), 123
"The Flame," Robert Laurent, 125
"Berg, 1909," Wassily Kandinsky, 129

Creating a percussion composition 73
Irregular meter 80
MELODY IN MUSIC 84
Step pattern of the major scale 88
The minor scale 90
HARMONY IN MUSIC 95
Harmony with chords 97
Harmony with parallel thirds 100
EXPRESSION IN MUSIC 104
Tempo 106
Dynamics 109
Articulation 110
The Mikado 112

THE STRUCTURE OF MUSIC 119

BALANCE IN MUSICAL FORM 120
Musical cadence 130
A song puzzle 135
The ostinato 138
Making music with ostinatos 146
VARIATION IN MUSIC 148
Melodic variation 150
Rhythmic variation 158
Creating musical variations 166

Works of Art
"Region of Brooklyn Bridge Fantasy,"
   John Marin, 132
"Gelmeroda," Lyonel Feininger, 137
"Frauenbildnis," Oskar Kokoschka, 137
"Umbrellas in the Rain," Maurice B.
   Prendergast, 138
"Flags on the Pavilion," Paul Klee, 146
"Brass Band," John Covert, 153
"Trees and Barns, Bermuda," Charles
   Demuth, 155
"Architectural Cadences," Charles
   Sheeler, 157

"Dance Rhythms," Abraham Walkowitz, 1970
Painted Chest, New Mexico, 173
"Dancers at the Bar," Edgar Degas, 176
"Lobster Fishermen," Marsden Hartley, 202

Art Activities
Voiceprints, 13
Contrasts in shape and color, 15
Creating with "found objects," 31
Repeated patterns, 35
Collage, 80
Shape and color, 88
Moods in painting, 93
Contrasts, 94

MUSIC AND DANCE 169
Folk dance 170
Theater dance 177
Music, drama, and dance: The opera 182
Amahl and the Night Visitors 183

THE PERSPECTIVES OF MUSIC 203

WHAT MAKES MUSIC "POPULAR"? 204
Where does popular music come from? 206
Keeping a record of popular songs 212

THE MUSIC OF EARLY AMERICA 213

MUSIC OF THE EUROPEAN NOBILITY 227
The Age of Bach 228
The Age of Haydn and Mozart 236

SONGS FOR FOUR SEASONS 241

MUSIC OF MY COUNTRY 269

MORE CHORAL MUSIC 277

PLAYING THE UKULELE 294

DO YOU KNOW? 317

GAME TIME 320

SAY IT WITH MOVEMENT 322

GLOSSARY OF TERMS 325

Indexes 328

Works of Art
"Still Life with Crystal Bowl," Roy Lichtenstein, 210
"Conversation Piece: William and
 Mary," J. N. Eaton, 217
"The Talcott Family," Deborah Goldsmith, 217
"String Quartet," Max Oppenhiem, 237
"Roitschäggäte" (Swiss mask), 244
"Road with Cypress and Stars," Vincent
 Van Gogh, 247
"Adoration of the Kings," Jan Brueghel, 257
"Adoration of the Shepherds," Rembrandt,
 261
"Washington at Verplanck's Point,"
John Trumbull, 268
"Guernica," Pablo Picasso, 273

Art Activities
Abstract drawing, 99
Using art components, 132
Drawing with ink, 137
Crayon etching, 147
String pictures, 153
Contracts with lines, 155
Variations in drawing, 168
Painting with rhythm, 170
Creating a stained glass painting, 266

Philadelphia Museum of Art. Louise and Walter Arensberg Collection. Photo by A. J. Wyatt.

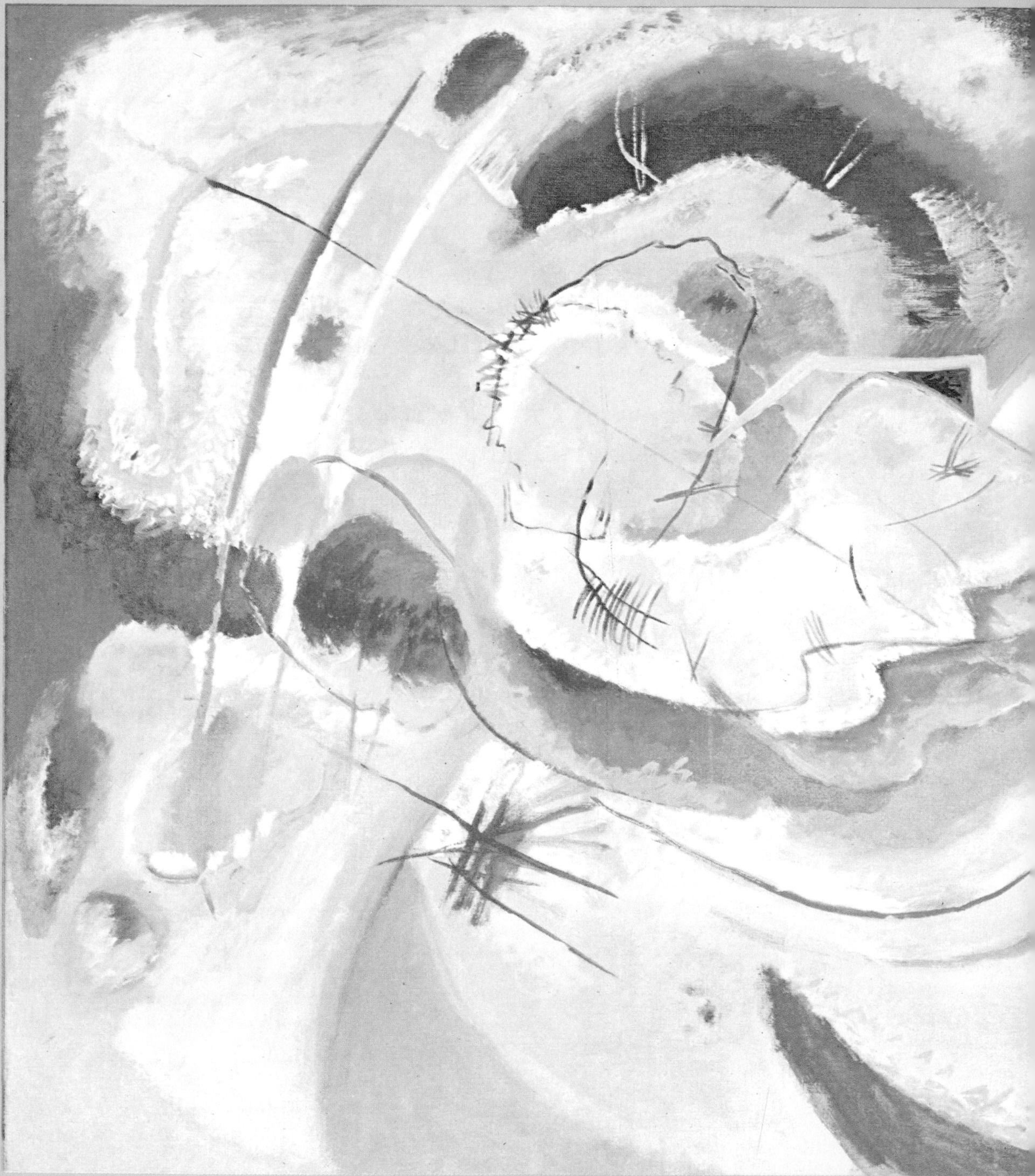

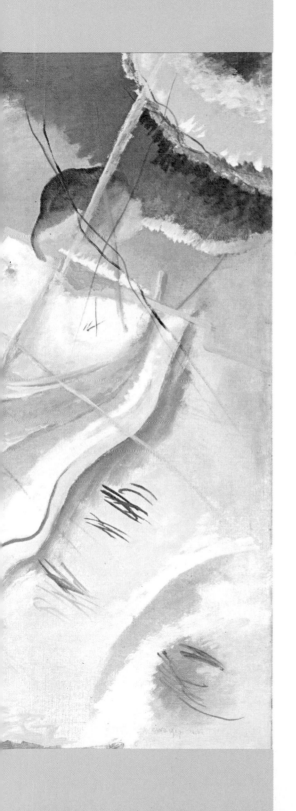

The media of music

Voices and instruments, alone or together, are called the media of music. Instrument makers, composers, and performers are constantly looking for ways to change and improve the sounds of instruments. New media are always being developed.

There are many tools and materials which can be used to create art: crayon and chalk, paint mixed with water or oil, electricity, and even things we would ordinarily throw away. What did the artist use to create his work?

Learning about voices

There are many kinds of voices. Every voice has its own tone quality or **timbre.**

The voices of young people have a certain timbre.

The voices of adults have a certain timbre.

Some women's voices sound high and light.

Some women's voices sound low and heavy.

Some men's voices sound high and light.

Some men's voices sound low and heavy.

The voice is a very special musical instrument. People are able to express many feelings and ideas with their voices.

What idea does "This Is My Country" express?

This Is My Country

Music by Al Jacobs
Words by Don Raye

Expressing feelings through song

Your voice is different from any other voice. Although no two voices sound exactly the same, all voices can express the same feelings. How can you use your voice to express the feeling of this song?

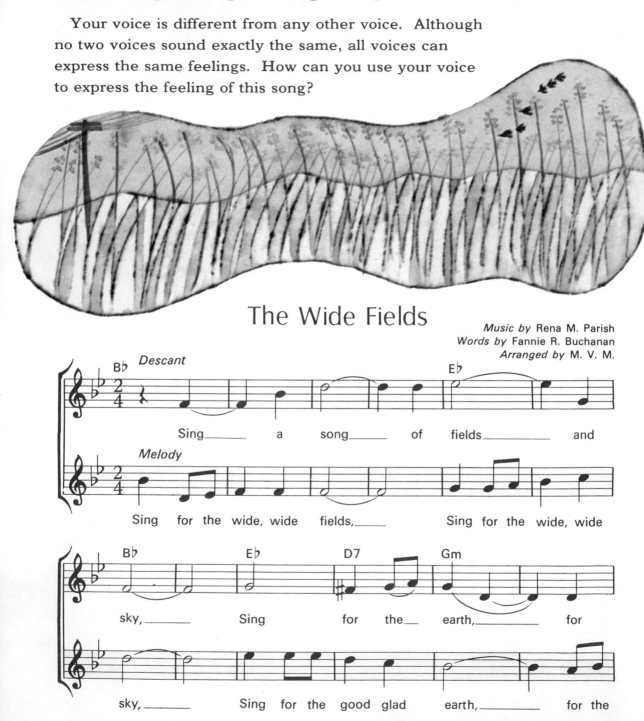

The Wide Fields

Music by Rena M. Parish
Words by Fannie R. Buchanan
Arranged by M. V. M.

Descant: Sing_____ a song_____ of fields_____ and

Melody: Sing for the wide, wide fields,_____ Sing for the wide, wide

sky,_____ Sing for the_____ earth,_____ for

sky,_____ Sing for the good glad earth,_____ for the

Artists can express what they feel and think by using different media. The type of media artists choose helps them express their ideas. Think of many different kinds of art media. What are some of the feelings and ideas that can be expressed through each of them?

Each medium is often used in different ways by different artists. For example, look at the paintings of farm scenes by two artists who used the same medium—oil paint. In what ways did these two artists use their brushes and paint differently?

7

Each verse of "I'm Gonna Sing" expresses a different feeling. Some of the verses are full of excitement. Others are quiet. Use your voice in different ways to express the feeling of each verse.

I'm Gonna Sing

Spiritual
Arranged by John Northrup

I'm gon-na sing, sing, sing,_____

I'm gon-na sing when the Spir-it says "Sing,"_____

And o-bey the Spir-it of the Lord._____

And o-bey the Spir-it of the Lord._____

2. I'm gonna shout when the Spirit says "Shout," (*3 times*)
   And obey the Spirit of the Lord.

3. I'm gonna preach when the Spirit says "Preach," (*3 times*)
   And obey the Spirit of the Lord.

4. I'm gonna pray when the Spirit says "Pray," (*3 times*)
   And obey the Spirit of the Lord.

5. I'm gonna sing when the Spirit says "Sing," (*3 times*)
   And obey the Spirit of the Lord.

"Sing Your Way Home" is a good song to sing on a hike. It is arranged for two voice parts. At the beginning of the song, the melody is in the lower voice part. Near the end of the song, the melody is in the higher voice part, and the harmony is in the lower voice part.

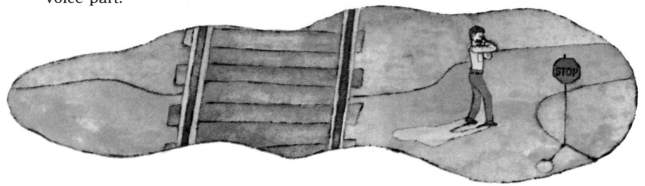

Sing Your Way Home

Traditional
Arranged by Cynthia Gordon

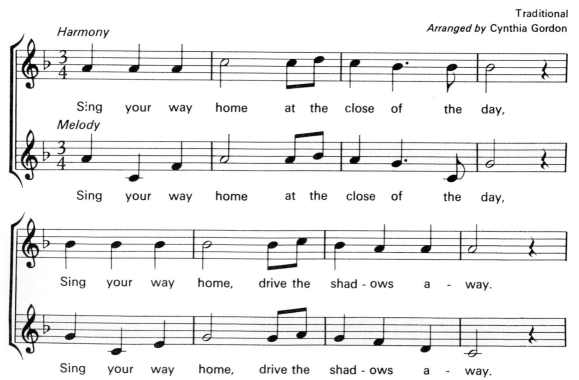

Harmony

Sing your way home at the close of the day,

Melody

Sing your way home at the close of the day,

Sing your way home, drive the shad - ows a - way.

Sing your way home, drive the shad - ows a - way.

Smile ev - 'ry mile, for wher - ev - er you roam

Smile ev - 'ry mile, for wher - ev - er you roam

Melody

It will bright - en your road, It will light - en your load,

Harmony

It will bright - en your road, It will light - en your load,

If you sing your way home.

If you sing your way home.

11

The Tortilla Man
(*El Tortillero*)

Chilean Folk Song
English Text by Kurt Johnson

Hot tor - ti - llas! Crisp to - sta - das!
No - che o - scu - ra, na - da ve - o

They're the best in Mex - i - co. Hot tor -
Pe - ro lle - vo mi fa - rol; Por tus

ti - llas! Crisp to - sta - das! Will you buy be -
puer - tas voy pa - san - do, y can - tan - do

fore I go? How man - y tor - ti - llas
con a - mor. Mas, voy can - tan - do

will you buy from me? Who'll buy my
con har - ta pe - na. ¿ Quien com - pra

hot tor - ti - llas? Who'll buy them from me?
mis to - sta - das? ¿ Tor - ti - llas bue - nas?

Your speaking voice

Each speaking voice has its own timbre and its own
range (highness or lowness). Speaking voices also use
dynamics (degree of loudness and softness).

The print of the sound of a person's voice is as
individual as his fingerprint. This is a picture of two
voice prints. The two people were making the same
sounds, but the pictures of their voices are very different.

Think of two people you know. How would you describe
the differences in their voices?

Courtesy of Voiceprint Laboratories, Somerville, New Jersey.

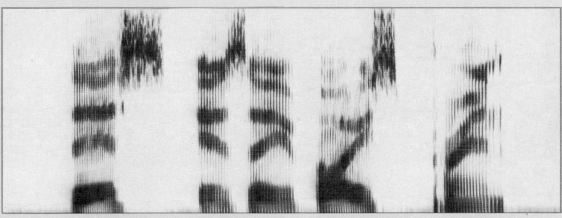

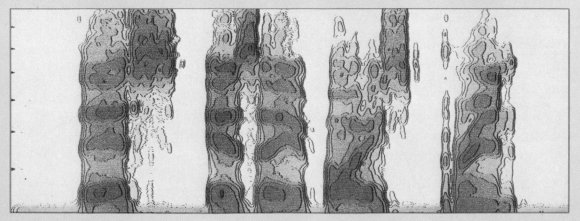

Some compositions use only the speaking voice.
"Crossroads of America" is a composition for spoken
voices. Begin by reading the words in the rhythm given.

Crossroads of America

C. A. R.

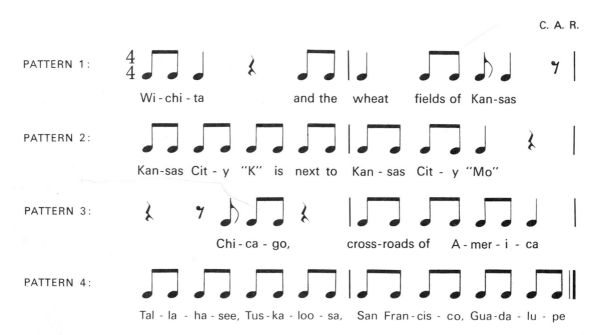

You may combine the patterns in "Crossroads of
America" in many different ways.

1. Read the patterns as a round. You may remember
   that in a round voices sing the same music, but start
   at different times.

2. Work in four groups. Each group repeats one of the
   patterns. A conductor could decide when each
   pattern will start and stop.

3. Read the patterns with changing dynamics.
   See the chart on page 15.

The Cleveland Museum of Art, Mr. and Mrs. William H. Marlatt Fund.

This painting by John Rogers Cox is called "Grey and Gold." It is a painting with strong contrasts. Describe the contrasts in shape and color. You can make contrasts in your own paintings by doing the following things with watercolors and brushes.

1. Use plenty of water for light, dull colors. Use very little water if you want bright, intense colors.

2. Use a dry brush as you paint. This may make interesting textures.

3. Press the brush; then lift it almost off the paper for a thick-thin line.

Geographical Fugue
Ernst Toch

"Geographical Fugue" is a composition for speaking chorus. The chorus is divided into four voice parts: soprano, alto, tenor, and bass. The composition begins with these words.

Trinidad! and the big Mississippi and the town
Honolulu and the lake Titicaca, the Popocatepetl is
not in Canada, rather in Mexico, Mexico, Mexico.

Listen to the composition and answer these questions.
1. Which voices enter first?
2. In what order do the other voices enter?
3. What plan was used for the dynamics in the composition?
4. In what order are the loud sounds and the soft sounds of the music heard?

After listening to "Geographical Fugue," plan another performance of "Crossroads of America." You may wish to use ideas from "Geographical Fugue."

Your singing voice

Each singing voice has its own range and its own timbre. A person can be identified by his voice range and timbre, just as he can be identified by his physical appearance. Why is it easy to tell a man's voice from a woman's voice?

When boys and girls are young, their singing voices sound very much alike. These voices are called **unchanged voices.** Between the ages of twelve and sixteen, people's voices begin to change. Boys' voices become lower in pitch and are called **changed voices.** Girls' voices often become fuller in sound, although the changes in their voices are not as noticeable.

Voices are classified by their range and timbre.

WOMEN'S VOICES

Soprano
The highest voice. The soprano voice has a bright quality.

Mezzo-soprano
A voice that sounds between the soprano and alto in range. The mezzo-soprano voice has a rich quality and a bright tone.

Contralto (usually shortened to "alto")
A voice that is lower in range than the mezzo-soprano. The contralto voice is rich and full, especially in the lower part of its range.

MEN'S VOICES

Tenor
The highest of men's voices. The quality of a tenor voice may be dramatic and rich, or it may be light.

Baritone
A voice that is richer in sound and lower in pitch than the tenor.

Bass
The lowest of all voices. The bass voice has a deep, full sound.

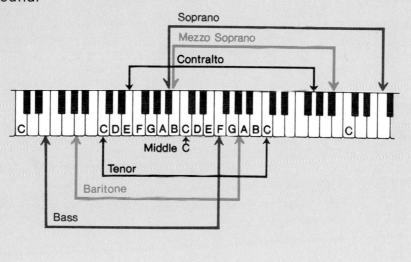

Check your voice range. How low and how high can you sing? Keep a record of your voice range to see if there is a change from month to month.

Record your voice on a tape recorder. Listen to it. How would you describe the quality of your voice?

light	warm	deep
soft	rich	thin
heavy	bright	raspy

The sound of the cuckoo is a sign of spring in many
parts of Europe. "The Winter Now Is Over" tells of the
cuckoo's message.

On your recording, a tenor sings the melody of this song.
A soprano sings the higher part, or **descant.** The soprano
and tenor voices blend well. How would you describe
the difference in the sound of the two voices?

The Winter Now Is Over

Italian-Swiss Folk Song
Descant by C. A. R.

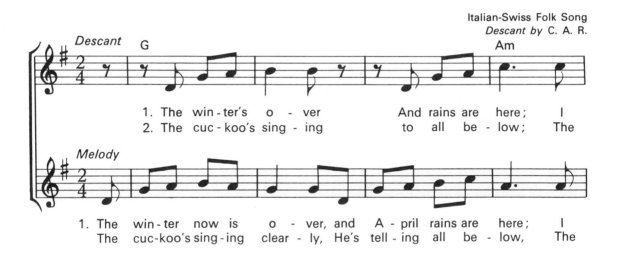

1. The win-ter's o - ver And rains are here; I
2. The cuc-koo's sing-ing to all be - low; The

1. The win-ter now is o - ver, and A - pril rains are here; I
The cuc-koo's sing-ing clear - ly, He's tell-ing all be-low, The

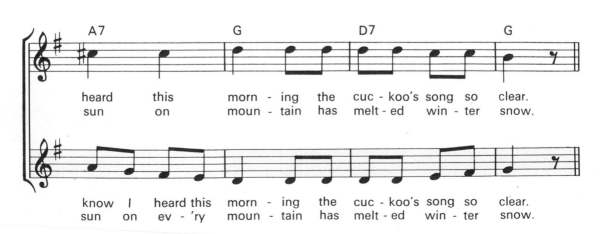

heard this morn - ing the cuc - koo's song so clear.
sun on moun - tain has melt - ed win - ter snow.

know I heard this morn - ing the cuc - koo's song so clear.
sun on ev - 'ry moun - tain has melt - ed win - ter snow.

Refrain

Cuc-koo! Cuc-koo! Oh, hear it too?
{ I
  The

Cuc-koo! Cuc-koo! Oh, can't you hear it too?
{ I
  The

heard this morn - ing the cuc - koo's song so clear.
sun on moun - tain has melt - ed win - ter snow.

know I heard this morn - ing the cuc - koo's song so clear.
sun on ev - 'ry moun - tain has melt - ed win - ter snow.

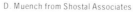

The photographer of this picture chose this view to express the mood of spring-time. Are the colors in the photograph similar, or are they contrasting? What color is the most obvious? Why do you think the photographer included the snow-capped mountains in the picture?

"The Shrimp Girl" by the English painter William Hogarth is a bright and radiant painting. How did Hogarth use his paint and brushes to create such a happy work of art? What makes this a happy painting?

A baritone sings the melody of this American folk song on your recording. How would you describe the sound of the baritone voice?

Black Is the Color

Appalachian Folk Song

Black, black, black is the col-or of my true love's hair.

Her lips, her eyes are won-drous fair,

The pret - ti - est face and the dain - ti - est hands.

I love the ground where-on she stands.

He Shall Feed His Flock from THE MESSIAH
George Frederic Handel

An **oratorio** is a composition for solo voices, chorus,
and orchestra. An oratorio is usually based on a religious
topic. An oratorio, like an opera, tells a story. Usually,
however, an oratorio is performed without costumes,
scenery, and stage action.

Handel, in his famous oratorio *The Messiah,* wrote the aria
"He Shall Feed His Flock" for contralto and soprano.
An **aria** is a vocal solo with instrumental accompaniment.

The contralto sings the first part of the aria.

He__ shall feed his flock like a shep - - herd,

The soprano sings the second part, beginning with the
words "Come unto Him . . . ." Notice that the soprano
solo uses almost the same melody as the alto, but the
soprano solo is written in a higher key.

come____ un - to Him,____ all ye that la - bor

As you listen to the recording, think of how you might
describe the difference between the sound of the alto
voice and the sound of the soprano voice.

This is an etching by the great Dutch artist Rembrandt. An etching is made by coating a sheet of copper or other metal with a thin layer of wax. A sharp tool is then used to scratch lines into the wax. Acid is poured over the metal after the lines have been cut. The acid eats into the metal where the wax has been scratched away. The wax is then removed. Ink is applied to the metal plate. Some ink sinks into the etched lines; the extra ink is wiped off. Finally, paper is pressed over the metal plate and a print is made.

The adult soprano's voice and the boy soprano's voice have a similar range, but the timbres are different. This difference can be heard in the recording of "Cockles and Mussels." The adult soprano sings the melody. The boy soprano sings the descant.

Cockles and Mussels

Irish Folk Song
Arranged by C. A. R.

Fresh cock - les !_____ Fresh mus - sels !_____ Fresh cock - les !_____

A - live, a-live oh! 1. In Dub-lin's fair cit - y, where girls are so pret-ty,
2. She was a fish-mon-ger, but sure, 'twas no won-der,
3. She died of a fe - ver and no one could save her,

I first set my eyes on sweet Mol - ly Ma - lone,
For so were her fa - ther and moth - er be - fore;
And that was the end of sweet Mol - ly Ma - lone;

As she wheeled her wheel - bar-row through streets broad and nar - row,
And they wheeled their wheel - bar-row through streets broad and nar - row,
Now her ghost wheels her bar-row through streets broad and nar - row,

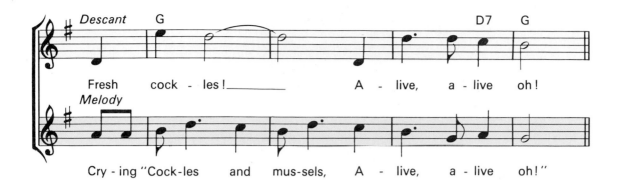

Descant — G — D7 G

Fresh cock - les !_____ A - live, a - live oh!

Melody

Cry - ing "Cock-les and mus-sels, A - live, a - live oh!"

Refrain G — D7

Fresh cock - les !_____ Fresh mus - sels !_____

A - live, a - live oh!__ A - live, a - live oh!__

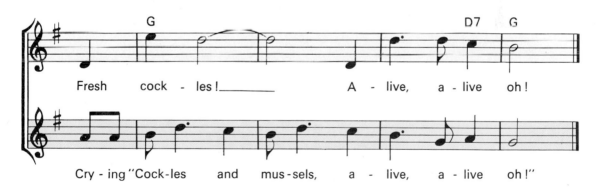

G — D7 G

Fresh cock - les !_____ A - live, a - live oh!

Cry - ing "Cock-les and mus - sels, a - live, a - live oh!"

Describe the difference in the sounds of the two voices. How do the singers create a contrast in mood between the first two verses and the final verse? How will you create a difference in mood when you sing this song?

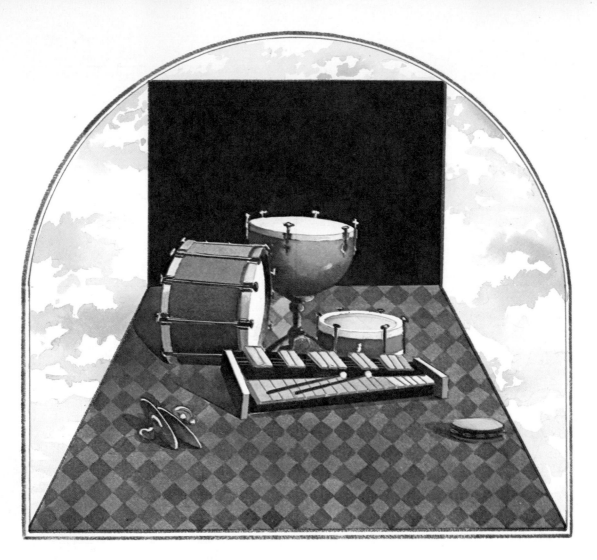

Exploring
percussion instruments

Percussion instruments are very important in today's music. They provide rhythm and a variety of tone color. Listen to almost any recording of popular music, and you will hear percussion instruments. Some music has been written for percussion instruments alone. A percussion performer is called a **percussionist**.

OCTOBER MOUNTAIN, Second and Fourth Movements
Alan Hovhaness

   October Mountain is a set of five short pieces written
by the American composer, Alan Hovhaness. The music
is written for marimba, glockenspiel, timpani, tenor
drum, bass drum, gong, and tam-tam.

   The marimba is very important in the first piece you
will hear. Listen to the recording.

Alfred Fisher

Describe the way the marimba
is used in this music. How are the other
instruments used? What instruments are most
important in the second piece you hear?

CREATE YOUR OWN PERCUSSION MUSIC

You can compose music with percussion instruments.
First you will need a plan. Your music may be composed as
you play it, that is, improvised. The following ideas may be
helpful in developing your music.

1. Work in **quintets.** (A quintet is a five-member group.)
   Everyone should make suggestions for the piece.

2. One person may play the bells, piano, or another tuned
   instrument. He may select three or four different pitches
   and play continuously. This will give unity to
   the composition.

3. The other performers may select four percussion
   instruments of contrasting timbres. This will give
   variety to the composition. The players should decide
   where in the music each of the instruments will play.

4. Plan for the dynamics.

Perform the composition. Make a tape recording of the
performance. Listen to the tape and discuss what made
the composition interesting. Suggest some ways that it
might be improved.

Many objects that you see every day can be used as art media. Leaves, rocks, nails, buttons, and tree bark can be art media. Above is the way an American artist used "found objects" to make a work of art.

Make a grouping of several objects. What materials might you use together to produce contrast? Combine objects you have found in such a way that they no longer appear to be leaves, rocks, nails, or buttons.

31

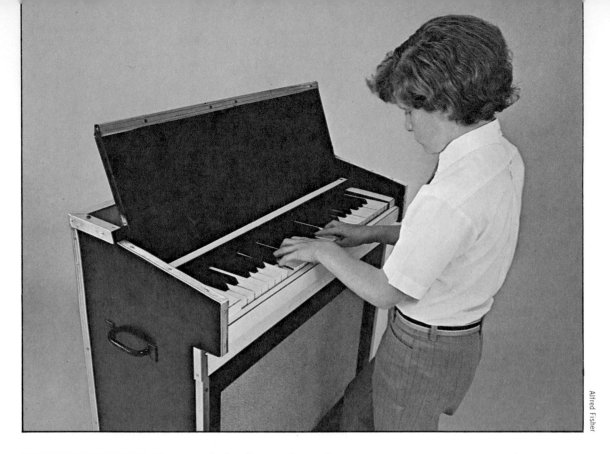

Alfred Fisher

LISTENING
Dance of the Sugarplum Fairy
from THE NUTCRACKER SUITE
Peter Ilyich Tchaikovsky

The **celesta** is a keyboard percussion instrument. It looks like a small piano. Inside the celesta are small hammers. When the keys are pressed, the hammers strike small metal bars. Tubes beneath the bars make the sound louder.

Tchaikovsky chose the celesta to play "Dance of the Sugarplum Fairy" in his ballet *The Nutcracker Suite.* Listen to the delicate, bell-like sound of the celesta in this composition.

32

Sketch for Percussion
Ronald Lo Presti

"Sketch for Percussion" is a composition with many contrasts. What musical contrasts can you name that are used in this music?

On some percussion instruments the sound can be sustained by a fast repeated striking. This repeated striking with mallets is called a **roll**. If two different pitches are struck repeatedly, a **trill** results. Examples of rolls and trills are heard in "Sketch for Percussion."

The following percussion instruments are used in the composition.

piano	xylophone	timpani	triangle
celesta	marimba	snare drum	suspended cymbal
		bass drum	gong

Listen to the recording. Identify the instruments as they are heard in the music. Which instruments play sustained sounds? Which instruments play rolls? Which instruments play trills?

Alfred Fisher

As you sing the words of "Johnny Morgan" you will probably agree that his band was very special. Create a percussion accompaniment for the refrain (the part of the song that is repeated after each verse).

Johnny Morgan

American Dance Tune
Traditional Words

1. I'll sing of a band that used to play mu - sic in the street,
2. They used to___ say that John - ny was the smart-est of them all,
3. Now one day___ John, he chanced to play out-side a la - dy's door,

And if you heard it, you would say it was an - y - thing but sweet.
And round the a - rea win - dows he would of - ten make a call.
And the la - dy said she'd nev - er heard such_ mu - sic played be - fore.

They all played diff - 'rent in - stru-ments, the mu - sic was the same,
His mu - sic was so live - ly, all the lat - est airs from France,
It pleased her so that you must know, she quite large sums would pay

And they were all one fam - i - ly, and Mor-gan was their name.
The ser - vant girls could not keep still, and mu - sic made them dance.
If he would stand out - side the house and play to her all day.

Refrain:

Johnny Morgan played the organ, the father beat the drum,

The sister played the tambourine, The

brother went pum, pum, pum, pum, pum.

All alone on an old trombone, the music was so sweet,

They often got a penny to go off to another street.

Many interesting designs can be found on wallpaper, textiles, and wrapping paper. When looking at designs, the eyes move from one repeated unit to another. Design some patterns with shapes or lines suggested by different word patterns.

Repeat some of your patterns on a large piece of paper. You might also combine two or more patterns. Cut shapes from paper, and use paint for line patterns. Some designs will be suitable for wrapping paper. Some would be better for a fabric. How could your design be used?

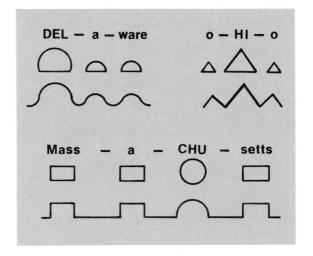

CREATING MORE PERCUSSION MUSIC

You might create your own "Sketch for Percussion." Use sharp contrasts in sound. The following plan may help.

1. Work in **quartets.** (A quartet is a group of four.) Everyone should suggest ideas for the composition.

2. Select four percussion instruments with contrasting timbres.

3. Explore each instrument. Try to find ways of playing sustained sounds and short sounds.

4. Develop a plan in which both kinds of sounds are used.

5. Use contrasts in volume and contrasts between sound and silence.

6. Chart your ideas on paper to help you remember the order of sounds during the performance.

7. After the composition has been planned, perform it.

8. Record your composition on a tape recorder. Listen to the recording and evaluate it.

Discuss the composition. What did you like about the music? How could you change the composition to make it more interesting?

Exploring strings

There are many kinds of stringed instruments. Name the instruments in this picture. What are some ways they can be played?

Vigolin

German Folk Tune
English version by Marilyn Keith and Alan Bergman

1. We   know of   a man   with a   lit-tle vi - o - lin,   and he plays his vi - o - lin
2. Now, no - bod - y   knows that the   lit-tle vi - o - lin   is   a   ma - gic vi - o - lin

Where-ev - er   he   does   go.   Where - ev - er   he   does   go,
No,   no - one knows but   he.   No,   no - one knows but   he

un - der-neath his dou - ble   chin   is   his lit - tle   vi - o - lin._____
that the   lit - tle vi - o - lin   is   a ma - gic   vi - o - lin._____

And he fid - dles a friend-ly   tune all day, A   hap - py man is   he.
For the tune that it plays makes a boy and girl_____ prompt-ly fall in   love.

Vi - go - lin, vi - go - lin, vi - go, vi - go - lin,

Vi - go - lin, vi - go - lin, vi - go, vi - go - lin.

Just lis-ten to his tune and Ver-y, ver-y soon you will find your-self in love.

Vi - go, vi - go, vi - go - lin. Vi - go, vi - go, vi - go - lin.

On the recording, which part of the song is sung by
men's voices only? What instruments are played to
accompany the singers?

Violinists and **cellists** can play in orchestras or with string ensembles. Outstanding violinists and cellists play in recitals and as soloists.

Sometimes violinists and cellists play in concerts for pay. Other times they play just for the fun of it.

Many violinists and cellists play in string quartets. Some play for folk dances such as hoedowns. They are called "fiddlers."

To play well, one must have a good ear and be willing to study and practice. Good violinists and cellists are in demand for their services.

Frank Sileman/TAURUS PHOTOS, INC.

LISTENING *Choros No. 6-bis for Violin and Cello*
Heitor Villa-Lobos

Heitor Villa-Lobos was a famous South American composer. As a child, he studied music with his father. They played in restaurants and theaters to earn their living. Villa-Lobos was much interested in Brazilian folk music and traveled far into the jungle to find it.

In "Choros No. 6-bis for Violin and Cello," you hear many of the special sounds that stringed instruments can produce.

At the beginning of the composition the players touch two strings at once with their bows. When both the violin and the cello are played in this way, four pitches are heard. These make chords. Playing two tones at the same time is called playing **double stops.**

The instrumentalists play **arco** (by bowing) and **pizzicato** (by plucking).

You will hear the players slide their fingers up or down the strings. The sliding sound is called **glissando.**

You will also hear a thin, silvery sound. This sound is made by lightly touching the string with the left hand. The tones produced in this way are called **harmonics.**

40

Robert McBride is an American composer who has used Mexican folk songs in some of his compositions. McBride used the melody of the carol below in his *Fantasy on a Mexican Christmas Carol.*

Christmas Carol
(*Villancico de Navidad*)

Mexican Folk Song

In - fant so di - vine, O lit - tle Child so ten - der,

Joy - ful - ly we come and lov - ing - ly a - dore.

Praise be un - to God, As hom - age now we ren - der

Je - sus, ti - ny One, Whom now___ we kneel be - fore.

Heav'n's se - rene - ly gleam - ing, glo - rious - ly and bright,___

All the works of God are man - i - fest to - night.

Fantasy on a Mexican Christmas Carol
Robert McBride

In this composition, the sound of the orchestra is rich
and beautiful. Which of the following does McBride
include in his music?

strings only

strings with woodwinds

strings with brass and percussion instruments

Sometimes composers want their music to sound
smooth. Smooth, connected tones are called
legato tones.

Sometimes composers want the tones in their music
to sound short and separated from one another. Short,
separated tones are called **staccato** tones.

Is this music played legato or staccato?

What else makes this music interesting?

The harp

The harp is one of the oldest stringed instruments still in use today. The strings of the harp are stretched *away* from the sounding board and are attached to a neck. Modern harps have pedals which a player uses to change the pitches of the strings.

The harp has been popular for centuries in Ireland and Wales. It is often used to accompany folk songs such as "The Ash Grove." This is a quiet Welsh song that tells of a favorite childhood place.

The Ash Grove

Welsh Folk Song

The ash grove, how_ grace-ful, how plain - ly__ 'tis__ speak - ing,
Where - ev - er the__ light through its bran - ches_ is__ break - ing,

The harp through it__ play - ing has lan - guage for me;
I see the__ kind__ fa - ces of friends dear to me.

The_ friends of__ my__ child - hood a - gain are__ be - fore me,

Each step brings a__ mem - ory as free - ly I roam;

With soft whis - pers_ speak - ing, its leaves rus - tle__ near me.

The ash grove, the__ ash grove a - lone is my home.

The symphony orchestra

A symphony orchestra includes many different
instruments. Do you know where to look for each group
of instruments when you go to an orchestra concert or
see an orchestra on television?

This chart shows one of the standard seating plans for the instruments of the orchestra. Sometimes, however, a different seating plan is used.

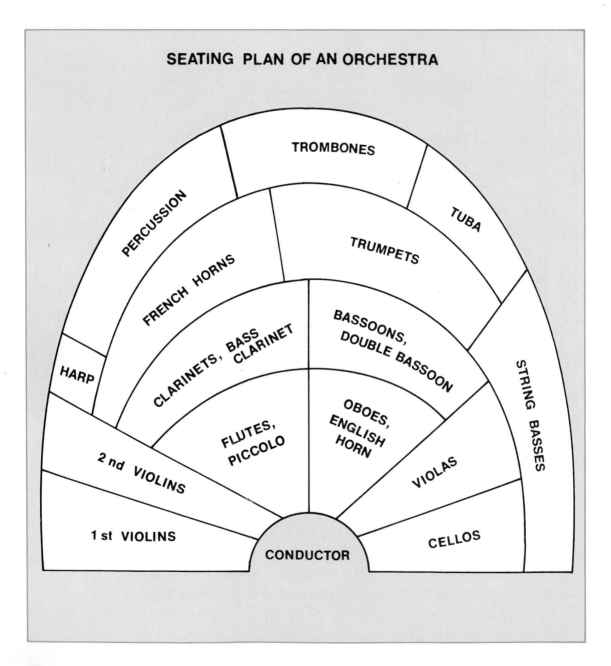

SEATING PLAN OF AN ORCHESTRA

Many composers have used familar folk songs when writing music. Georges Bizet, who wrote *L'Arlésienne Suite No. 1,* used an old French song to begin his music.

LISTENING *Overture (excerpt) from L'ARLÉSIENNE SUITE NO. 1*
Georges Bizet

Georges Bizet presents the "March of the Three Kings" as a melody with four variations.

Melody   The orchestra plays the melody with strong accents.

Variation 1   The woodwinds play in a smooth style.

Variation 2   The woodwinds and brass play the melody. The strings play rapid scales.

Variation 3   The cellos play the melody. The French horn and bassoon can be heard in the background.

Variation 4   The full orchestra plays the melody.

LISTENING *Farandole from L'ARLÉSIENNE SUITE NO. 2*
Georges Bizet

The farandole is a French dance. Bizet used a farandole melody in his *L'Arlésienne Suite No. 2.*

What other melody do you hear in this composition? Create your own dance to this lively melody.

Bizet used an ancient French carol, "March of the Three Kings," to begin the overture of his *L'Arlésienne Suite No. 1.* An **overture** is music written as an introduction to an opera, an oratorio, a musical play, a ballet, or a suite.

March of the Three Kings

French Carol

Three great kings___ I met at ear - ly morn,___ With all their
Ce ma - tin,___ J'ai ren-con-tré le train___ De trois grands

Three great kings___ I met at ear - ly morn,__ With
Ce ma - tin,___ J'ai ren - con-tré le train__ De

ret-in-ue were slow - ly march-ing; Three great kings_ I met at ear - ly
Rois qui al-laient en voy - a - ge, Ce ma - tin,___ J'ai ren-con-tré le

all their ret-in-ue were slow-ly march-ing; Three great kings___ I
trois grands Rois qui al-laient en voy - a - ge, Ce ma - tin,___ J'ai

morn,_____ were on their way to meet the new - ly born.
train_____ De trois grands Rois des-sus le grand che - min.

met at ear - ly morn,___ to meet the new - ly born.
ren - con-tré le train___ des-sus le grand che - min.

With gifts of gold brought from far a - way,_____
Tout char - gés d'or les sui - vaient d'a - bord_____

And val - iant war - riors to guard the king - ly trea - sure.
De grands guer - riers et les gar - des du tré - sor,_____

With gifts of gold brought from far a - way,_____
Tout char - gés d'or les sui - vaient d'a - bord_____

And shields all shin - ing in their bright ar - ray.
De grands guer - riers a - vec leurs bou - cli - ers.

Composers often combine melodies. In "The Instruments," five melodies can be sung at the same time. Each melody represents the sound of an instrument. Think about the sound of each instrument. Imitate its timbre as you sing.

The Instruments

Music by Willy Geisler
Words by Julius G. Hereford

The vi - o - lin's ring - ing like love - ly___ sing - ing.

The clar-i-net, the clar-i-net makes doo-dle, doo-dle, doo-dle, doo-dle det.

The trum-pet is bray-ing ta ta ta ta ta te ta, ta ta ta ta ta te ta.

The horn, the horn a - wakes me at morn.

The drum's play-ing two tones and al - ways the same tones;

The vi - o - lin's ring - ing like love - ly song.

The clar-i-net, the clar-i-net makes doo-dle, doo-dle doo-dle det.

The trum - pet is bray - ing, ta ta ta ta ta te ta, ta ta ta ta.

The horn, the horn a - wakes me at morn.

Five, one, one, five, five, five, five, five, one.

F7   Bb

Knowing the score

An orchestral score is like a road map which helps the conductor guide the musicians through a musical composition. The score contains the notation for each instrument of the orchestra. It helps the conductor decide such things as the appropriate dynamics, tempo, accents, and phrasings.

The first page of an orchestra score is shown on page 53.

LISTENING | *Piece 4 from* FIVE PIECES FOR ORCHESTRA, *Op. 10*
Anton Webern

Piece 4

from *FIVE PIECES FOR ORCHESTRA, Op. 10*

by Anton Webern

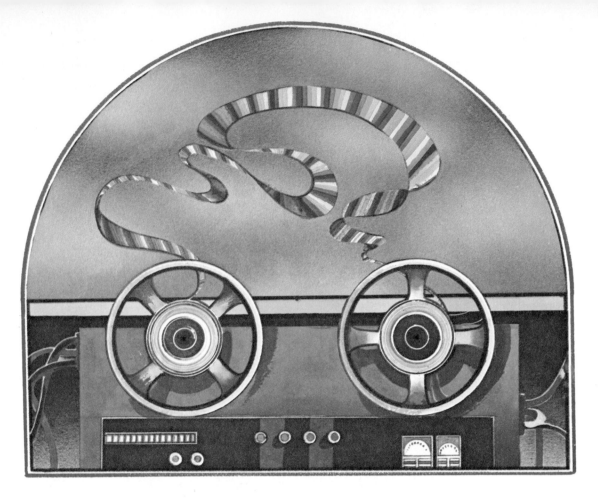

Exploring music
with tape recorders

One of the most exciting developments in music in
recent times has been the growth in the use of electronic
media. The sounds of guitars and other instruments
have been amplified electronically. Electronic pianos
and organs have been produced. Special devices such as
the **synthesizer** have offered new sounds to composers
and performers. The synthesizer is a set of tone-generators,
filters, and electronic switches that can produce practically
any sound or combination of sounds the composer desires.

Improvisation for Solo Performer and 5 Tape Recorders
Georg Polski

The tape recorder was one of the first electronic instruments used by composers. Listen to what one composer has created with several tape recorders.

Alfred Fisher

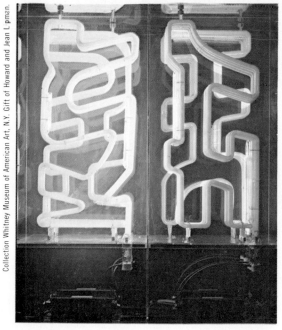

Collection Whitney Museum of American Art, N.Y. Gift of Howard and Jean Lipman.

Electricity has become an important medium for the artist. Electric motors can be used to make sculptures move. Electricity makes it possible to produce colors that flash and move to form exciting patterns.

How could you construct an object that changes its appearance as it moves?

COMPOSING WITH TAPE RECORDERS

If you know how to operate a tape recorder, you can create a composition of your own.

I. Securing sounds

A. Select a sound source. This might be a telephone, doorbell, typewriter, or any object that is capable of making two or more different tones.

B. Record each sound in a variety of different ways:
1. with the microphone at a normal distance from the object,
2. with the microphone touching the object,
3. at the slowest tape speed,
4. at the fastest tape speed,
5. with the volume control very high.

II. Playing back sounds

A. Play back the tape and identify each sound. Describe the pitch, timbre, volume, and duration of each sound.

B. Play back the tape at different speeds. Describe the changes in pitch, timbre, volume, and duration of each sound.

C. Experiment with the volume controls. What is the effect of a crescendo or a decrescendo? What is the effect of a sudden volume change?

D. Experiment with the interruption of sound by using the pause lever or the on-off switch.

III. Creating tape loops

    A. Select from the tape a sound you wish to use as a continuous background. Cut out that part of the tape. Use a splicing block, or cut the ends of the tape at the angle shown. Splice the ends of the tape together to make a continuous loop.

    B. Place the loop in the tape recorder. Play the tape and practice the controls described in Step II.

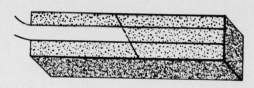 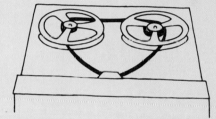

IV. Composing with the tape loops

    A. Use three or four tape recorders, one to record the composition and the others to play the loops.

    B. Choose a composer-conductor to organize the sounds, or follow this plan:

        1. Use one tape loop for a continuous sound. (This will give unity to the composition.)

        2. Use the other tape loops for occasional sounds. (These will give contrast to the composition.)

        3. Plan the way dynamics are to be varied. Make a chart showing the order of soft and loud sounds. Your chart could also show the times when each loop will be silent and when each will be heard.

        4. Record the composition according to the plan.

Oven Grill Concerto
Americole Biasini and Lee Pogonowski

Did you ever think of an oven grill as a musical instrument? The sounds in this composition are all produced on an oven grill. The composers fastened two sides of the grill to the microphones with string. They played the oven grill with their hands and with a variety of mallets. A tape recorder with an echo was used to record the sounds.

The Electric Room

Click, silence, fling, flick,
Ding, bing,
         Perma Press.

Gargle, slosh, bang, click,
Sizzle, ring,
         "Hello. Yes."

Whish, whee, zzzzz, whirr.
Taste, turn, time, touch.
Zing, wiggle, sip, zirr.
"Quiet day, nothing much."

Susan Lucas

"The Electric Room" may give you some ideas for a
composition. The music might be made with vocal sounds,
or the sounds might be played on percussion instruments.
A composition could also be created by recording each
of the sounds mentioned in the poem.

The components of music

Music is made of sounds. Anyone can enjoy music just by listening to it. But people can enjoy music even more when they understand it, and when they can recognize its components.

The components of music are rhythm, melody, harmony, and expression. A composer uses these components in many different ways.

The components of art are line, color, shape, value, and texture. Artists use the components of art to achieve various effects in their works.

Rhythm in music

You can see a flute, but you can't see its sound. Sound exists in time. Each sound has a beginning and an end. The length of time each sound exists is its **duration**.

Sounds of various duration are grouped together to make **rhythm**.

This song is sung by a cowboy in Chile. He sings about his white horse, who is his faithful friend.

Mi Caballo Blanco

Chilean Folk Song

Es mi ca - ba - llo blan - co com - o un a - man - e - cer,

Siem - pre jun - ti - tos va - mos, es mi a - mi - go mas fi - el.

Mi ca - ba - llo, mi ca - ba - llo, se va y se va

Mi ca - ba - llo, mi ca - ba - llo, se va y se va.

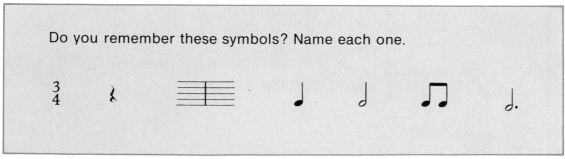

Do you remember these symbols? Name each one.

The men who built the first railroads in America worked
hard and long. These men were sometimes called
"tarriers." "Drill, Ye Tarriers" tells about some of the
hardships these men faced.

Drill, Ye Tarriers

Music *by* Charles Connoly
Words *by* Thomas Casey

1. Oh, ev - 'ry morn-in' at sev - en o' clock,__ There's a
2. Now, our new fore-man was Jer - ry Mc - Cann,__ You can
3. Now, next time pay - day come__ a - round,__ Jim__

hun - dred tar - ri - ers a - work - in' at the rock And the
bet that he was sure a blame__ mean__ man, Last__
Goff a dol - lar__ short__ was__ found, When__

boss comes a - long and he says, "Keep still! And
week a__ pre - ma - ture__ blast went off, And a
asked what__ for, came__ this re - ply, You were

come down heav - y on the cast iron drill, and
mile in the air___ went___ big Jim Goff, and
docked for the time___ you were up in the sky! So

Refrain

Drill, ye tar - ri - ers, drill. Drill, ye tar - ri - ers, drill.

Oh, it's work all day for sug - ar in your tay,

Down be - hind the rail way, Oh, drill, ye tar - ri - ers, drill!"

Look at the music of "Drill, Ye Tarriers." Notice that the song begins with part of a measure rather than a complete measure. Look at the end of the song. The last measure is also incomplete. If you put the beginning and ending notes together, they make up a complete measure. The first note of the song is called a **pick-up note.**

The meter signature for "Drill, Ye Tarriers" is $\frac{2}{2}$. You may remember that this means there will be two counts in each measure (♩ ♩). The music notation in $\frac{2}{2}$ meter looks just like the notation in $\frac{4}{4}$ meter, but a song in $\frac{2}{2}$ meter usually moves a little faster than one in $\frac{4}{4}$ meter. Another symbol for $\frac{2}{2}$ meter is ¢ . This meter is often called **cut time.**

"Morning" is a four-part round. Learn the melody well before singing the song as a round. Sing the round in two parts. Then sing it in four.

Morning

Words and music by Isaac Woodbury

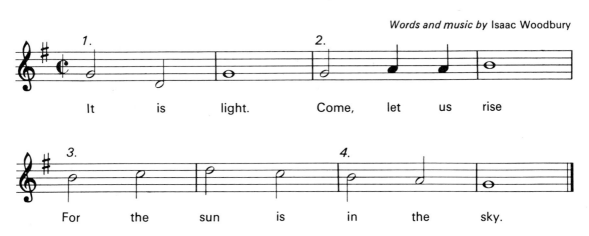

It is light. Come, let us rise

For the sun is in the sky.

Rhythmic lines guide the eyes in the picture "Two Cats" by Franz Marc. The general shape created by the lines is an oval. Trace around the lines of the picture with your finger. You will probably start with the blue cat. You can guide your finger smoothly around the picture.

The artist has repeated several shapes and colors in the picture. Where do you find them?

MUSICAL ARITHMETIC

Look at these rhythm phrases. One measure in
each phrase does not have the correct number
of counts.

1. Find the incomplete measure. (Remember, the
   top number of each meter signature tells how
   many counts should be in each measure. The
   bottom number tells what kind of note should
   be given one count.)

2. Decide what kinds of notes could be added to
   the incomplete measures to make them correct.

Rhythm patterns

One of the great songs of the United States is the "Battle Hymn of the Republic." This song was sung by the soldiers of the Union Army during the Civil War.

Battle Hymn of the Republic

Music by William Steffe
Words by Julia Ward Howe

Mine eyes have seen the glo - ry of the com - ing of the Lord;

He is tram - pling out the vin - tage where the grapes of wrath are stored;

He has loosed the fate - ful light - ning of His ter - ri - ble swift sword;

His truth is march - ing on.

"Battle Hymn of the Republic" is made up almost entirely of dotted rhythms. A dotted rhythm is made up of a dotted note plus a shorter note. A dot makes a note longer. It adds half the value of the note to itself. Study the chart below. It shows different kinds of dotted patterns.

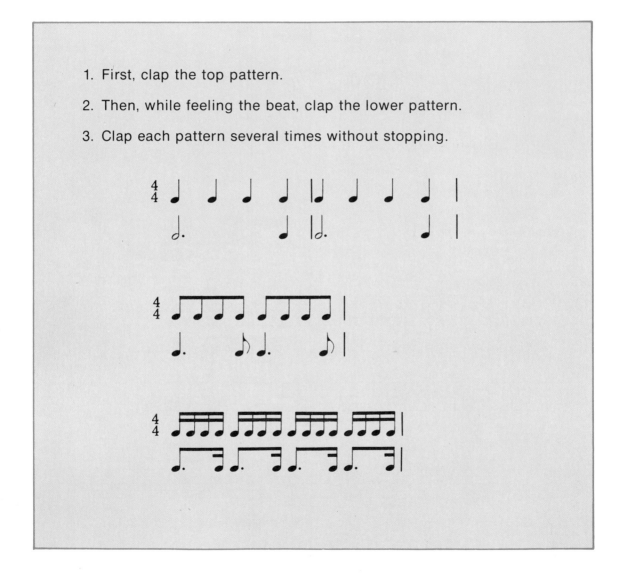

1. First, clap the top pattern.

2. Then, while feeling the beat, clap the lower pattern.

3. Clap each pattern several times without stopping.

Dotted patterns make **uneven rhythm.** Find dotted rhythms in other songs. Clap these rhythms.

The painting "Rhythm of a Russian Dance" has many rectangular shapes and several colors. What is the feeling of this picture? If you were to do a similar picture of the "Battle Hymn of the Republic," what shapes would you use? What feeling would you try to achieve?

71

Baby Elephant Walk
Henry Mancini

"Baby Elephant Walk" was composed as background music for a movie. In one scene of the movie, three baby elephants decide to take a walk into town. As you listen to the recording of "Baby Elephant Walk," listen for the dotted rhythm.

The painting by Rousseau is about a jungle. The row of trees behind the lion and the repeated shapes of the grass give rhythm to the picture. Look for other shapes that are repeated. Is there variety in this jungle or is it a dull place?

CREATING A PERCUSSION COMPOSITION

Words have their own rhythm patterns. You may have to listen carefully to find these patterns. When you speak your name, you are sounding a rhythm pattern.

Say your full name several times without stopping. Say it naturally. Listen to the rhythm of your name. Clap the rhythm. Find the parts of your name that are accented.

The class might make up a percussion composition based on names. Here are some ideas.

1. Choose four names that have different rhythm patterns.

2. Decide how to write these patterns in music notation.

3. Clap the patterns to hear their sounds. Then experiment with different ways of combining the patterns.

4. Choose a different percussion instrument to play each pattern.

5. Choose a fifth instrument to play a metric beat for your composition. This instrument should play an introduction to set the tempo.

6. Write a score of your composition. Be sure there is a line of the score for each part that is played.

7. Play your composition. There should be five performers and a conductor.

Long John Green was a prisoner. The sheriff wanted to test his new pack of bloodhounds. He sent Long John out to mark a trail for the dogs. But Long John was smart. He crawled through a vinegar barrel to cover his scent, and ran far away. The sheriff never found Long John Green.

"Long Gone," a tree-chopping song, tells the story of Long John Green. The strong, repeated rhythm patterns of the song help the workers chop wood at a steady pace.

Long Gone

American Folk Song

Leader: With his dia - mond blade, Got it in his hand, _
Chorus: With his dia - mond blade, Got it in his hand, _

Leader: Goin' to hew out the live oaks that are in this land. _
Chorus: Goin' to hew out the live oaks that are in this land. _

Leader: He's long gone. _ He's Long John. _
Chorus: He's long gone. _ He's Long John. _

Leader: He's gone, gone. _ Like a tur - key in the corn. _
Chorus: He's gone, gone. _ Like a tur - key in the corn. _

LONG GONE
Collected, Adapted and Arranged by John A. and Alan Lomax
TRO. © Copyright 1934 and renewed 1962. LUDLOW MUSIC.
INC.. New York, New York. Used by permission.

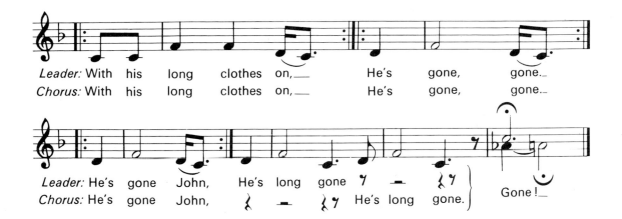

Leader: With his long clothes on,— He's gone, gone.—
Chorus: With his long clothes on,— He's gone, gone.—

Leader: He's gone John, He's long gone — Gone!—
Chorus: He's gone John, — He's long gone.

The repeat signs (‖: :‖) in "Long Gone" tell the chorus to repeat each part of the melody after the leader sings it.

Ralph Kleinhempel Hamburg.

The artist used similar shapes and colors to guide the eyes around the painting. Some shapes appear to be near; others seem far away. As you look at this painting, your eyes move to the back, to the front, and in a circle around the surface of the painting. By placing each color carefully, the artist made it easy for the viewer's eyes to move to all parts of the picture.

Mary Ann

Calypso Song

Refrain

F
All night, all day,___ Miss Ma - ry Ann,_____

Down by___ the sea - side,___ sift - ing sand._____

C7
Ev - ery - bod - y down there___ join the band,_____

F
Down by___ the sea - side___ sift - ing sand._____ *Fine*

Verse

C7
If you come to our Port of Spain, you'll nev - er want___ to go

F   Gm
home a - gain.___ You'll do ev - er - y - thing you can,___

C7   F   *D.C. al Fine*
Just to be___ round Miss Mar - y Ann.___

76

"Mary Ann" is a **calypso.** Calypso music comes from the island of Trinidad. It is a combination of African and Spanish music. The words to calypso songs are often improvised.

The people of Trinidad like to improvise (make up) rhythmic accompaniments for their calypso songs. They use many kinds of drums as well as other percussion instruments.

Find objects in your classroom that can be used to play rhythms. Use these to improvise various rhythm patterns as an accompaniment for "Mary Ann." Improvise other verses for the song.

Listen to the recording of "Mary Ann." It will help you learn to play and sing the calypso rhythms.

Souvenir de Porto Rico
Louis Moreau Gottschalk

Louis Moreau Gottschalk was the first American pianist
and composer to become famous in other countries. He
gave concerts in Europe and North and South America.

Gottschalk grew up in New Orleans about 150 years
ago. He loved the folk music he heard as a boy and used
folk tunes and rhythms in his own compositions.

In "Souvenir de Porto Rico," listen for this rhythm.
It comes a few moments after the music begins.

It is the rhythm of the cakewalk, a dance that was popular
in New Orleans when Gottschalk was a boy.

Find these two themes in the music as you listen.
What happens to the themes as they are repeated?

Theme 1

Theme 2

Listen to the music again. Does the piece begin with
a simple rhythm or a complicated rhythm?

What happens to the rhythm near the end of the piece?
Does it stay simple or get more complicated?

How does the piece end?

Collection, The Museum of Modern Art, N.Y., Theatre Collection.

Irregular meter

Clap these rhythm patterns. This sign > shows **accent.** Make the accented notes stronger than the other notes.

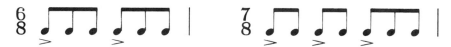

Which beats are accented in $\frac{6}{8}$ meter? Which beats are accented in $\frac{7}{8}$ meter?

A meter of $\frac{7}{8}$ is called **irregular meter** because it has an uneven grouping of beats within each measure.

Why is $\frac{6}{8}$ meter a **regular meter?**

The music of Greece, Yugoslavia, and Bulgaria often uses irregular meters. Play drums softly for an accompaniment to "Stoyan's Wife." Use the $\frac{7}{8}$ meter pattern shown above.

Artists sometimes use actual objects rather than painting representations of them. This type of art is called collage. This collage was made with stamps, bits of newspaper, and other materials.

Make a collage. Begin by collecting objects such as ticket stubs, buttons, pieces of cloth, paper clips, and stones. Use heavy paper as a background. Organize the objects into a pleasing design. Use similar shapes. Arrange the shapes so that the viewer's eyes move easily around the collage. When you have made an arrangement you like, glue the objects onto the heavy paper.

"Stoyan's Wife" is a folk tune from Yugoslavia. It should be sung gaily and at a fast tempo.

Stoyan's Wife

Yugoslavian Folk Song

1. Sto - yan, for to share his life,
2. Bake the bread she would not do,
3. Her the house - work did not please,

Sto - yan, for to share his life,
Bake the bread she would not do,
Her the house - work did not please,

Sto - yan, for to share his life,
Bake the bread she would not do,
Her the house - work did not please,

Chose a good, hard - work - ing wife.
Eat - ing it was all she knew.
As she'd rath - er take her ease.

4. Why should she of cooking think,
   Why should she of cooking think,
   Why should she of cooking think,
   When the milk was there to drink?

5. Stoyan, for to share his life,
   Stoyan, for to share his life,
   Stoyan, for to share his life,
   Chose a good, hardworking wife.

Freedom is precious. This song tells of the joy of
living in a place where everyone is free. The irregular
meter of this song seems to give the music a feeling
of freedom.

Man Must Be Free

Music by David L. Plank
Words by C. A. R.

Free, free as birds in the sky, you and I, like
leaves soft - ly flut - ter - ing by.

Now, now wher - ev - er we go, may we know that
man must al - ways be free, that

man must al - ways be free.

Look east or west, where peo - ple are blest and

there,   hap - pi - ness   will   grow._____

Joy,   joy   a - bounds in the   land,   fel - low - man,   come

let   your   love   ov - er - flow,_____   Come

let   your   love   ov - er - flow._____

83

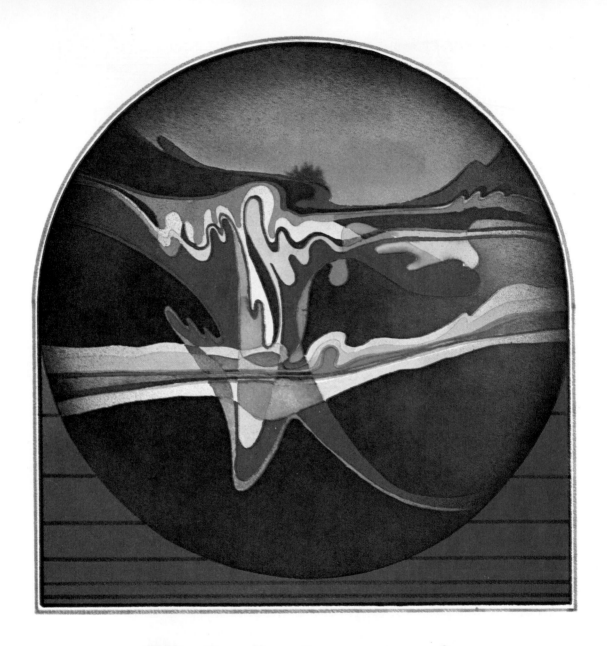

Melody in music

A melody is a group of pitches, heard one after the other. A melody also has rhythm. Each tone in a melody has pitch and duration.

Sometimes singing helps when a person is in trouble.

Nobody Knows the Trouble I've Seen

Refrain

Afro-American Spiritual

No-bod-y knows the trou-ble I've seen, No-bod-y knows my sor-row;

No-bod-y knows the trou-ble I've seen, Glo-ry hal-le-lu-jah.

Verse

Some-times I'm up, some times I'm down, Oh, yes, Lord! Some-
Al-though you see me goin' long so,

times I'm al-most to the ground, Oh, yes, Lord!
have my tri-als here be-low,   Lord!

Use this song to check your musical memory.
1. Name the notes in the melody.
2. An interval is the distance from one pitch to another.
   Find the intervals of a sixth, a third, and a second.

Here are three hints that can help you.

1.

2.

ABCDEFG

The Music Alphabet

3.

This is a sixth

Read this story. Then play the note patterns.

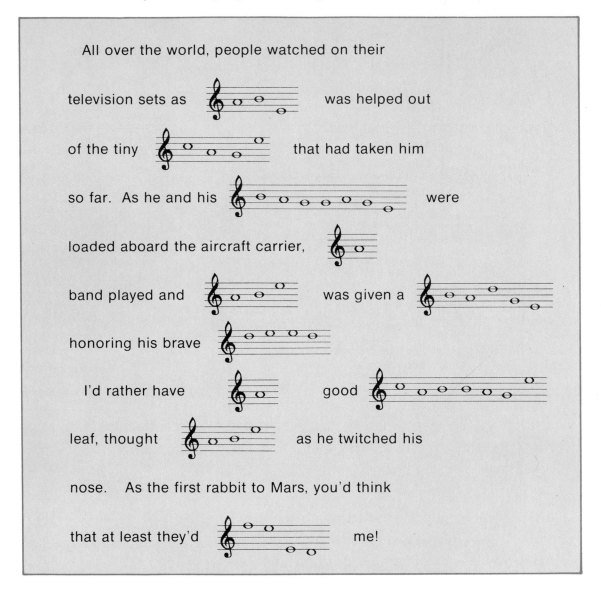

All over the world, people watched on their

television sets as ♪ was helped out

of the tiny ♪ that had taken him

so far. As he and his ♪ were

loaded aboard the aircraft carrier, ♪

band played and ♪ was given a ♪

honoring his brave ♪

I'd rather have ♪ good ♪

leaf, thought ♪ as he twitched his

nose.   As the first rabbit to Mars, you'd think

that at least they'd ♪ me!

There are more than fifty words which can be formed from the music alphabet (A B C D E F G). Make up a story of your own using words from the musical alphabet. First list as many of these words as possible. Then decide what your story will tell. Be careful to place your notes correctly on the staff. Ask someone to read your story.

"Never Argue with a Bee" contains some good advice. As you sing it, find and name the **accidentals**. Accidentals are sharps (♯), flats (♭), or naturals (♮) that are not in the key signature.

Never Argue with a Bee

Refrain

Words and music by Malvina Reynolds

Nev - er ar - gue with a bee. He has got a sting-a - ree.

Be he work-er, be he drone, You had best leave him a - lone.

1. He has got his work to do, Get-ting hon-ey from the tree.
2. And the wasp is ve - ry wild, If you both-er with his child;

If you know what's good for you, Do not ar - gue with a bee.
Let him go where he is bound, Do not try to mess a round.

How does the melody move? Look for places in the song where the notes are repeated, move by steps or half steps, and move by skips. When the melody moves by a skip, name the interval of the skip. The first skip is a fifth. What is the second skip?

STEP PATTERN OF THE MAJOR SCALE

Here is a picture of part of a keyboard.

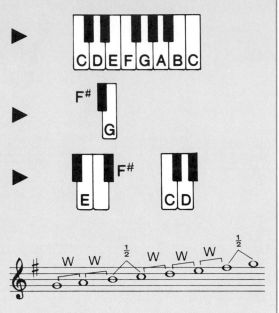

A half step is the distance from any key to its nearest neighbor. Play this half step. Listen to its sound. Then play other half steps.

A whole step is the distance of two half steps. Play these whole steps. Listen to their sounds. Play other whole steps.

You may remember that you can play a major scale beginning on any key of the piano or any bell, by using these whole (W) and half (½) step patterns.

Begin on G. Play the G major scale. It has one sharp. Which note has the sharp?

Make a picture by combining simple figures such as a bee and a tree. Use many shapes and sizes. Repeat some

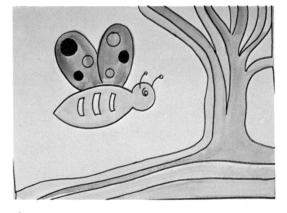

shapes. Color your work with one or two colors. Will you use warm or cool colors? Why?

The Man Who Has Plenty of Good Peanuts

American Folk Song

The man who has plen-ty of good pea-nuts, and giv-eth his neigh-bor none,
He shan't_ have an-y of my pea-nuts when his_ pea-nuts are gone.

When his pea-nuts are gone,_____ when his pea-nuts are gone.__ He

shan't have an-y of my pea-nuts when his pea-nuts are gone!_

Oh, that will be joy - ful, joy - ful, joy - ful!

Oh, that will be joy - ful, when his pea-nuts are gone!___

The key signature of this song has one sharp. This means that the song is in the key of G. It is based upon the G major scale.

The meter of this song is $\frac{6}{8}$. Is this regular or irregular meter?

The minor scale

"Shalom Chaverim" is a three-part round. The word "shalom" is used both as a greeting and as a goodbye. It means "Peace."

Shalom Chaverim

Israeli Round

Sha - lom,   good friends, Sha - lom,   good friends, Sha - lom,   Sha - lom!
Sha - lom,   cha - ve - rim,   Sha - lom   cha - ve - rim,   Sha - lom,   Sha - lom!

Till   once more we meet, till   once   more we meet, Sha - lom,   Sha - lom!
Le - hit - ra - ot,   Le - hit - ra   - ot,   Sha - lom,   Sha - lom!

This song is in a minor key. The pattern of intervals in a minor scale is different from that of a major scale.

Look at the two scales below. Notice that the key signatures are the same, but the scales start on different notes. The minor scale begins two scale steps lower than the major scale.

Play the two scales. Listen to the difference in their sounds. Play the first three notes of each scale. How are these first three notes different?

90

In the accompaniment to this song, you can hear sounds that suggest the gentle dripping of the raindrops. Sometimes music built on a minor scale sounds happy. Sometimes it sounds sad. The tempo of the music helps create a happy or a sad mood.

Rain

Words and music by Linda Leslie

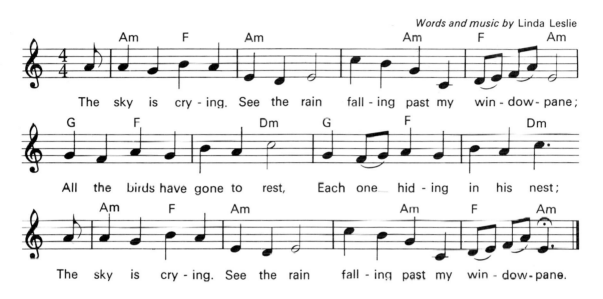

The sky is cry-ing. See the rain fall-ing past my win-dow-pane;

All the birds have gone to rest, Each one hid-ing in his nest;

The sky is cry-ing. See the rain fall-ing past my win-dow-pane.

The artist Charles Burchfield painted a picture called "Church Bells Ringing—Rainy Winter Night." How did the artist give his picture a feeling of dampness? Are the colors bright and cheerful, or dark and cold? Do the shapes move up or down? As you look at the picture, do you feel you are standing still or moving? Are you hunched over in your coat or standing up straight? How would you change the lines, shapes, and colors to paint "Church Bells Ringing—Bright Summer Day"?

Sometimes songs in minor keys sound gay and exciting.
When you have learned this song, play the tambourine
and finger cymbals to provide an accompaniment. Play
these rhythmic patterns or make up others.

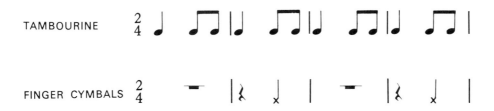

TAMBOURINE

FINGER CYMBALS

Let Us Sing and Rejoice

Hasidic Song

O let us sing,_____ Let us re - joice._____ O let us

O let us sing,_____ Let us re - joice._____

Fine

sing,_____ Let us re - joice.

_____ O let us sing,_____ Let us re - joice.

La   la   la la la la la   la   la la la la la_____ la.   La   la.

La   la la la   la la la la la la   la la la la la_____ la.   La   la.

Make up a melody. Use the tones of the E minor scale.
Begin and end your melody on E.

E   F♯   G   A   B   C   D   E

After you have composed your melody, add some words.
Choose words that express the same mood as your melody.
You might also compose an accompaniment for your
melody.

Make a painting which suggests the mood of the song you compose. Remember that many different sizes, shapes, and lines suggest activity. Complex shapes and slanting lines also suggest activity. Simple shapes and horizontal or vertical lines suggest inactivity. Warm colors are generally happy, gay, active. Cool colors suggest quiet, calm, rest.

"Lullaby" is neither sad nor happy. It is a quiet song a mother sings to soothe her baby. One accidental, F♯, occurs in this song. Sing the song without the accidental, then with it. Which version do you like better? Why?

Lullaby

Words and music by Charles Chandler

Hush, oh, hush - a - bye, Oh, my lit - tle one,

While the moon is shin - ing.

Hush, oh, hush - a - bye, Hush, now, do not cry,

Hear, the winds— are sigh - ing.

Look at the painting by Georgia O'Keeffe on page 60. This is very different from the Burchfield picture on page 91. In the O'Keeffe painting there are enough dark parts for contrast, but not enough to be bold. The shapes are large and simple, and the edges are soft. In contrast, the Burchfield painting has small shapes, sharp lines, and much contrast. How would you describe the mood of the O'Keeffe painting?

Harmony in music

Harmony is made by sounding different pitches at the same time. When a round is sung, or a descant is added to a melody, harmony is heard. There are many interesting ways to make harmony.

"Evening" was written long ago by the same person who wrote "Morning". These two rounds can be sung in several different ways. One way is to sing them at the same time. Try this. Then discover other ways to sing them to make harmony.

Evening

Words and music by Isaac Woodbury

1. Stars shin - ing o - ver - head 2. Tell us to go to bed.
3. Dear friends, good night; 4. Dear friends, good night.

Morning

Words and music by Isaac Woodbury

It is light. Come, let us rise
For the sun is in the sky.

Harmony with chords

Harmony is made with chords.

Chords are built on single tones called **chord roots.** When the third and fifth tones above any pitch are added, a **triad** is formed. Each triad is named for its root.

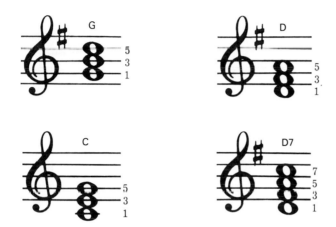

Look at the D7 chord. Notice that another note has been added to the D chord. This makes the harmony more interesting.

Play these chords on the bells to make harmony for "Evening."

Accompany the song with the autoharp. Listen to the sounds of the autoharp. How does this accompaniment sound different from the bell accompaniment?

One easy way to hear and to sing harmony is to
practice singing the chord roots.   Try this with "Go
Tell Aunt Rhody."

First sing the melody of the song.

Go Tell Aunt Rhody

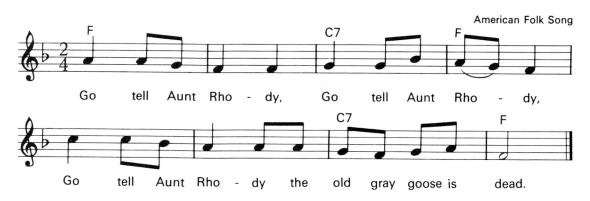

American Folk Song

Go   tell   Aunt   Rho - dy,   Go   tell   Aunt   Rho - dy,

Go   tell   Aunt   Rho - dy   the   old   gray   goose is   dead.

Then divide the class in half. Half of the class should
sing the melody, while the other half sings the chord roots below.

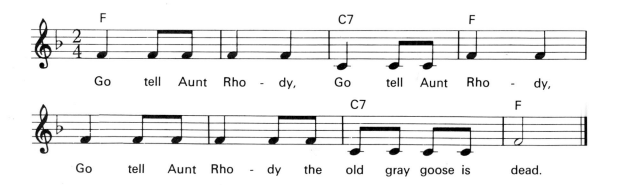

Go   tell   Aunt   Rho - dy,   Go   tell   Aunt   Rho - dy,

Go   tell   Aunt   Rho - dy   the   old   gray   goose is   dead.

Chord roots can also be played on bells, recorders, or
the piano.

"Camptown Races" is harmonized with three chords:
C, F, and G. First learn the melody, and then divide into
two groups and sing the song with chord roots to add
harmony. You might try humming the chord roots instead
of singing the words.

Camptown Races

Words and music by Stephen C. Foster

Camp-town la - dies sing this song, Doo - dah, doo - dah.
Went down there with my hat caved in, Doo - dah, doo - dah.

Camp-town race track five miles long, Oh, doo - dah - day.
Came back home with a pock-et-ful of tin, Oh, doo - dah - day.

Goin' to run all night, Goin' to run all day,

Bet my mon-ey on the bob - tailed nag, Some-bod-y bet on the bay.

It is fun to work on a picture with another person. Use a pencil and make an abstract line drawing that suggests fast or slow motion, of being heavy or soft, wet or dry. Exchange pictures with another person in class. Your classmate should paint the picture with colors that seem to fit the drawing.

Harmony with parallel thirds

"Haidschi, Bumbaidschi" is an Austrian lullaby. A mother is telling her baby to sleep well. She is going away, but the angels will watch over the little one.

The harmony for this song is written in **parallel thirds.** This means that the two parts will always be a third apart.

Listen carefully. Decide where each chord should be played. Sing one phrase at a time. Try the chords several times if you are not sure.

Haidschi, Bumbaidschi

Softly

Austrian Folk Song

1. Hush - a - bye,   lit - tle   ba - by,   sleep   well   now,
A - ber Haid - schi, Bum - baid - schi schlaf lan - ge,

Your moth - er   is   go - ing   a - way   now;
Es   ist   ja   dei-ne Mut - ter   aus-ge - gan - gen,

She is go - ing a - way____ so far, far from home
Sie____ ist ja aus-ge-gan - gen und kommt lan - ger nicht heim

But she will not leave her boy ba - by a - lone.
Und lässt das klei-ne Büb - chen al - lein nicht da - heim.

Refrain

A - ber haid - schi, bum - baid - schi, sleep well,____
A - ber haid - schi, bum - baid - schi, schlaf, wohl,____

A - ber haid - schi, bum - baid - schi, sleep well.____
A - ber haid - schi, bum - baid - schi, schlaf, wohl.

2. Hushabye, little baby, sleep sweetly,
   The angels so gently will greet thee.
   Will greet thee so gently, so gently and then
   They'll sing thee a song as they hover o'er head.
   Refrain

   Aber haidschi, bumbaidschi, schlaf süss
   Die Engelein lassen dich grüssen
   Sie lassen dich grüssen und lassen dich fragen
   Ob sie das kleine Bübchen umher sollen tragen.
   Refrain

Play an autoharp accompaniment for "Haidschi,
Bumbaidschi." Use the F and C7 chords. Listen
carefully. Decide where each chord should be played.

Béla Bartók was a Hungarian composer. He wrote many kinds of music. Bartók's music is exciting and is filled with bold harmonies and exciting rhythms.

This music is sometimes called "Game of Pairs." You have been studying the chords of the autoharp. Autoharp chords are built with intervals of thirds. Bartók's music contains some groups of thirds, and it also has groups of seconds, fourths, and fifths. Play some of these intervals on the bells or on the piano.

Find the answers to the following questions:

1. Which instrument is heard first?

2. Which instruments play the interval of a second?
   Play a second on the piano or bells.
   A second looks like this:

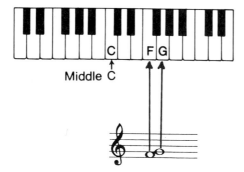

3. What makes the middle section sound different from the rest of the music? What type of instrument plays the middle section?

4. Which instrument ends the composition?

5. Why do you think this music is called "Game of Pairs."?

You have learned that harmony in art is achieved when all the components of a work go well together. Look at "Singing Man." The sculpture is made of bronze, and the surface is smooth.

The man is singing and the expression on his face is happy. The pose, the expression of the face, and the texture of the piece go well together. All the parts of this sculpture are in harmony.

103

Expression in music

Moonlight

Shhh! The moon-lady watches . . .

She sends her golden rays of light
To touch the quiet earth at night . . .

The night owl stares with eyes aglow
At shadows moving down below . . .

Night birds, silent, wing their way
As leaves in gentle breezes sway,

And fishes in the silver stream
Reflect the shining golden beam.

The moon-lady watches. She smiles . . .

Michael Chandler

Many stories and poems have been written about the moon. Read the poem "Moonlight" and think about the words. If you were to choose music to be played as a background while someone read the poem aloud, what kind of music would you choose?

Read "Moonlight" aloud. How should your voice sound? Should it be loud or soft? Should you read the words slowly or rapidly? Should you read smoothly, or should you say the words in a short, crisp manner?

In music, tempo (speed), dynamics (volume), and articulation (the way the tones begin and end) are sometimes called **expressive controls.** These are the same expressive controls that are used in speaking.

LISTENING *Clair de Lune, Arranged for Orchestra*
Claude Debussy

Listen to "Clair de Lune" by Claude Debussy. Find some of the ways he used expressive controls in this music.

Artists often use size, proportion, or scale as an expressive control. This electric plug is very large. Thus it becomes something to look at and think about. Why do you think the artist chose a common object, an electric plug, as the subject for a sculpture?

Tempo

The **metronome** is a mechanical device which can be set at various speeds. The speed at which it ticks or clicks gives the speed of the beat. A marking of ♩ = 60, for example, indicates 60 beats per minute. When music has no metronome marking, it may be more difficult to find an appropriate tempo.

Sometimes you will see tempo indications in Italian or English at the beginning of the music.

Largo	very slowly
Andante	not too slowly
Moderato	moderately
Allegro	fast
Presto	very fast

The conductor decides how fast to conduct a composition. A "fast" tempo means different speeds to different people, just as "fast" means eighty miles per hour to one driver and sixty to another.

When you compose, you will find a tempo that you think is best for your music. When others play or sing your music, they will know the exact tempo you intended if you have used a metronome marking.

Sing this song at different speeds. Decide upon a
tempo which seems best. Conduct the song at that
tempo. What words could you use to describe the
tempo you have chosen?

Morning Song
(Las Mañanitas)

Mexican Folk Song
Translated by Olcutt and Phyllis Sanders
Based on an English text by Janet E. Tobitt

With a morn - ing song we greet you As King Da - vid used to sing,
Es - tas son las ma - ña - ni - tas Que can - ta - ba el Rey Da - vid,

But his song was not as love - ly As is the mu - sic we bring.
Pe - ro no e - ran tan bo - ni - tas Co - mo las can - tan a - quí.

A - wake, then, O my be - lov - ed, A - wake, for the dawn is nigh;
Des - pier - ta, mi bien, des - pier - ta, Mi - ra que ya a -ma - ne - ció;

Now the birds are sweet-ly sing - ing, The moon has gone from the sky.
Ya los pa - ja - ri - llos can - tan, La lu - na ya se o - cul - tó.

The sign *D.C. al Fine* means to go back to the
beginning and end at *Fine.*

Collection of the Colorado Springs Fine Arts Center. Gift of Oliver B. James

"Fog Horns" has shapes and colors that give a feeling of sounds heard through the fog. The colors are soft and dull, suggesting stillness. The horns are suggested by uneven circular shapes. The color values of the circles change from dark in the center to light at the edges. This change in value suggests movement of the sound through the fog.

The components of this painting —the horizontal lines, the soft, dull colors, and the simple shapes—work together to give the impression of vagueness which one feels in a fog.

Dynamics

Just as it is sometimes difficult to tell how fast or slow music should be, it can also be difficult to decide what level of volume is most suitable.

Practice singing this song softly. Then try singing it even more softly. Which of the dynamic markings would you use? Look at the terms and markings on page 15. Change the volume several times during the song. Which of the terms and markings would you use? How would a conductor show the class when to sing louder or softer?

Night Mist

Music by Alan Phillips
Words by Ronald Smyth

The mist falls and cov-ers build - ings.

Soft - ly it drapes the streets with its fog-gy arms,___

and set-tles down to sleep un - til morn-ing awakes.

Articulation

The way in which a tone is begun and ended is called
articulation. Articulation is important in musical
expression.

What are some of the differences between the ways in
which a wood block and a violin are played? The wood
block player can only tap the instrument, but violinists
can begin and end sounds in several ways. They can
pluck strings or bow them.

Singers can begin and end tones differently also.
They can perform slow, smooth, legato tones or short,
staccato tones. Listen to "The Alphabet" to find the
staccato tones. How are they marked?

CAREERS

An **orchestrator** is a special kind of
composer. This person takes music and
arranges it to be played by various combinations of instruments and voices.
An orchestrator must know much
about music, instruments, and voices.

LISTENING *Syncopated Clock*
Leroy Anderson

The clock described in this music
is not an ordinary clock. Once in
a while it has a syncopated tick.
The tick occurs in an unexpected
place.

As you hear "Syncopated Clock,"
listen for the tones played by the
stringed instruments. Some of
them are staccato, some legato.
Compare the sounds of the stringed
instruments to those of the
wood block (the clock's tick).

The Alphabet

Music attributed to W. A. Mozart
Adapted by Zelma Putnam

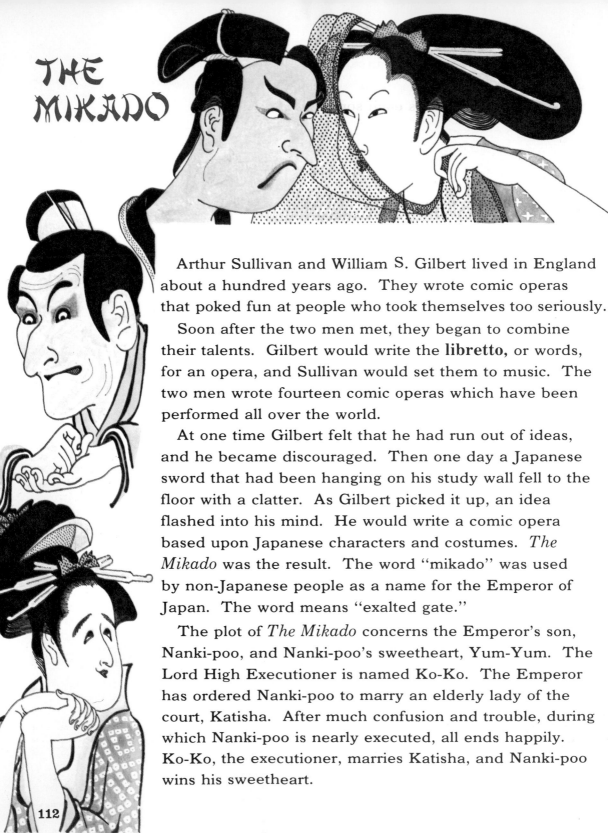

THE MIKADO

Arthur Sullivan and William S. Gilbert lived in England about a hundred years ago. They wrote comic operas that poked fun at people who took themselves too seriously.

Soon after the two men met, they began to combine their talents. Gilbert would write the **libretto,** or words, for an opera, and Sullivan would set them to music. The two men wrote fourteen comic operas which have been performed all over the world.

At one time Gilbert felt that he had run out of ideas, and he became discouraged. Then one day a Japanese sword that had been hanging on his study wall fell to the floor with a clatter. As Gilbert picked it up, an idea flashed into his mind. He would write a comic opera based upon Japanese characters and costumes. *The Mikado* was the result. The word "mikado" was used by non-Japanese people as a name for the Emperor of Japan. The word means "exalted gate."

The plot of *The Mikado* concerns the Emperor's son, Nanki-poo, and Nanki-poo's sweetheart, Yum-Yum. The Lord High Executioner is named Ko-Ko. The Emperor has ordered Nanki-poo to marry an elderly lady of the court, Katisha. After much confusion and trouble, during which Nanki-poo is nearly executed, all ends happily. Ko-Ko, the executioner, marries Katisha, and Nanki-poo wins his sweetheart.

The next few pages contain songs from *The Mikado*.
Before singing each song, read the words. Think about
the character who sings each song in the opera. Then
decide on a suitable tempo, on dynamic levels, and
on the type of articulation you think will best fit the song.

This is the song the chorus sings as Ko-Ko, the Lord
High Executioner, comes on stage for the first time in
the opera. He is splendidly dressed. A small boy walks
before him carrying a ceremonial sword.

Behold the Lord High Executioner

Music by Arthur Sullivan
Words by William Gilbert

Chorus:

Be-hold the Lord High Ex - e - cu - tion-er! A per-son-age of no-ble rank and ti - tle, A dig - ni-fied and po - tent off - i-cer whose func-tions are par-tic - u - lar-ly vi - tal! De - fer,___ De - fer,___ To the Lord High Ex - e - cu - tion-er! De - fer,___ De - fer___ to the no - ble lord, to the no - ble lord, to the Lord High___ Ex - e - cu - tion - er!

Ko-Ko must marry Katisha and convince her to forget Nanki-Poo. In the song "Oh, Willow," Ko-Ko tries to persuade Katisha that he cannot live without her.

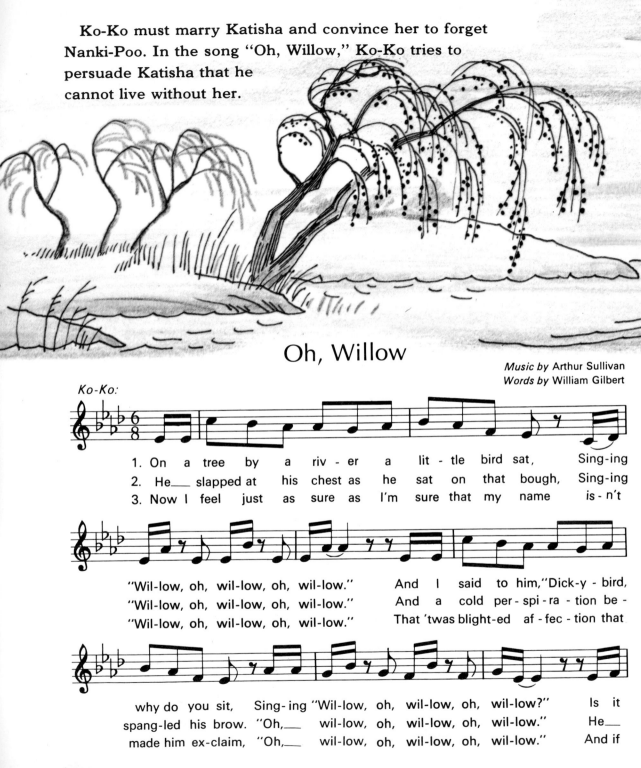

Oh, Willow

Music by Arthur Sullivan
Words by William Gilbert

Ko-Ko:

1. On a tree by a riv-er a lit-tle bird sat, Sing-ing
2. He__ slapped at his chest as he sat on that bough, Sing-ing
3. Now I feel just as sure as I'm sure that my name is-n't

"Wil-low, oh, wil-low, oh, wil-low."   And I said to him,"Dick-y - bird,
"Wil-low, oh, wil-low, oh, wil-low."   And a cold per-spi-ra - tion be -
"Wil-low, oh, wil-low, oh, wil-low."   That 'twas blight-ed af-fec - tion that

why do you sit, Sing-ing "Wil-low, oh, wil-low, oh, wil-low?"   Is it
spang-led his brow. "Oh,__ wil-low, oh, wil-low, oh, wil-low."   He__
made him ex-claim, "Oh,__ wil-low, oh, wil-low, oh, wil-low."   And if

114

weak-ness of in - tel-lect, bird - ie?" I cried, "Or a rath - or tough worm in your
sobb'd and he sigh'd and a gur-gle he gave, Then he plunged him-self in - to the
you re-main cal-lous and ob - du-rate, I shall___ per - ish as he did, and

lit - tle in - side?" With a shake of his poor lit - tle head he re - plied, "Oh,
bil-low - y wave, and an ech - o a - rose from the Su - i-cide's grave, "Oh,
you will know why. Though I prob - a-bly shall not ex - claim as I die, "Oh,

wil - low, oh, - wil - low, oh, - wil - low."___
wil - low, oh, - wil - low, oh, - wil - low."___
wil - low, oh, - wil - low, oh, - wil - low."___

Nanki-poo sings of his delight about his recent marriage, but Ko-Ko is not nearly as happy when he thinks of Katisha as a bride.

The Flowers That Bloom in the Spring

Music by Arthur Sullivan
Words by William Gilbert

Nanki-Poo: The flow - ers that bloom in the spring, Tra - la,
Ko-Ko: The flow - ers that bloom in the spring, Tra - la,

Breathe prom - ise of mer - ry sun - shine.
Have noth - ing to do with the case.

As we mer - ri - ly dance and we sing, Tra - la!
I've got to take un - der my wing, Tra - la,

We wel - come the hope that they bring, Tra - la,
a most un - at - trac - tive old thing, Tra - la,

Of a sum-mer of ros-es and wine. Of a sum-mer of ros-es and wine.
with a car - i - ca ture of a face, with a car - i - ca-ture of a face.

And that's what we mean when we say that a thing
And that's what I mean when I say or I sing,

is wel - come as flow - ers that bloom in the spring,
"Oh, both - er the flow - ers that bloom in the spring,"

Tra la la la la, _____ Tra la la la la, _____

The flow - ers that bloom in the spring. Tra la la la la, _____

Tra la la la la, _____ Tra la la la la la la!

The structure of music

The components of music are combined in many ways to build a piece of music. Each piece of music has form, or structure.

A musical structure is balanced by repetition and contrast. Think of an example of musical repetition in a song you know. Think of an example of musical contrast.

This painting has many different shapes, colors, and lines. These are repeated in various parts of the picture. By repeating these art components, the eyes move easily around the painting. This helps hold the picture together.

Seagram Building

Robert Doisneau from Rapho Guillumette Pictures.

Balance in musical form

Repetition helps give balance to music. There are many kinds of musical repetition.

The pictures above show two types of structures. Each structure looks like one unit. Each structure appears to be balanced. Visual balance helps unify a work. How do you think balance is achieved in each of these structures?

Where do you find repetition in "Sourwood Mountain"?

Sourwood Mountain

Appalachian Folk Song

1. Chick-en crow-in' on Sour-wood Moun-tain, } Hey de-ing dang did-dle al-ly day.
2. My true love's a blue-eyed dai-sy }

So man-y pret-ty girls I can't count them. } Hey de-ing dang did-dle al-ly day.
If I don't get her I'll go cra-zy, }

My true love she lives in Letch-er, } Hey de-ing dang did-dle al-ly day.
My true love lives in the hol-low, }

She won't come and I won't fetch her, } Hey de-ing dang did-dle al-ly day.
She won't come and I won't fol-low, }

Look at the four phrases of this song. Each line is a phrase. Now look at the groups of letters below. Each letter stands for a phrase. Which of the following groups of letters shows the phrase form of this song?

AABB   ABAB   ABAC

Sometimes repetition is found in the melodic rhythm.
(The melodic rhythm is the rhythm of the melody.)

Which phrases of the song "I'm on My Way" have
the same melodic rhythm?

I'm On My Way

Afro-American Spiritual
Words Adapted by Venoris Cates

1. I'm on my way _____ And I won't turn back! _____
2. I'm on my way _____ to the Free-dom Land! _____

I'm on my way _____ and I won't turn back! _____
I'm on my way _____ to the Free-dom Land! _____

I'm on my way _____ and I won't turn back! _____
I'm on my way _____ to the Free-dom Land! _____

I'm on my way, ___ My Lord, I'm on my way. _____
I'm on my way, ___ My Lord, I'm on my way. _____

3. I asked my brother to come with me,
   I asked my brother to come with me,
   I asked my brother to come with me,
   I asked my brother, My Lord, to come with me.

Find the repeated rhythm pattern in "La Calle Ancha."

La Calle Ancha

Puerto Rican Folk Song

1. La ca-lle an-cha, cha, cha de San Ber-nar-do, do, do,
2. Los cua-tro ca-ños, ños, ños dan a-qua her-mo-sa, sa, sa,

Tie-ne u-na fuen-te, te, te, con cua-tro ca-ños, ños, ños.
Pa-ra los ni-ños, ños, ños, de Za-ra-go-za, za, za.

Peggy Guggenheim Foundation, Venice.

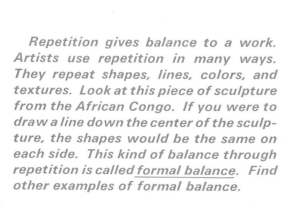

Repetition gives balance to a work. Artists use repetition in many ways. They repeat shapes, lines, colors, and textures. Look at this piece of sculpture from the African Congo. If you were to draw a line down the center of the sculpture, the shapes would be the same on each side. This kind of balance through repetition is called formal balance. *Find other examples of formal balance.*

What kinds of repetition are used in "Come and Dance"?
What keeps the repetition in the verse from
becoming monotonous?

Listen to each phrase of the verse. Where do you
hear contrast?

Come and Dance

Slovakian Folk Song
Words adapted by M. V. M.

Come and dance with stamp-ing and turn - ing, But

watch the stove or it may stop burn-ing, For

win - ter winds will chill us to - mor - row, And

there's no oth - er stove we can bor - row.

Refrain

La la la la la la la la

la la la la la la la la

Repetition is often found in the rhythmic movement of a work of art. Look at the sculpture "The Flame." One cannot divide this piece in half with a line, yet it looks balanced. The lines move in, out, and up like flames. The repetition of curved lines gives this piece balance and unity. "The Flame" has _informal balance_. If we were to divide the sculpture in half, the sides would "feel" as though they were the same weight. In formal balance, the sides are the same. Look for other examples of informal balance.

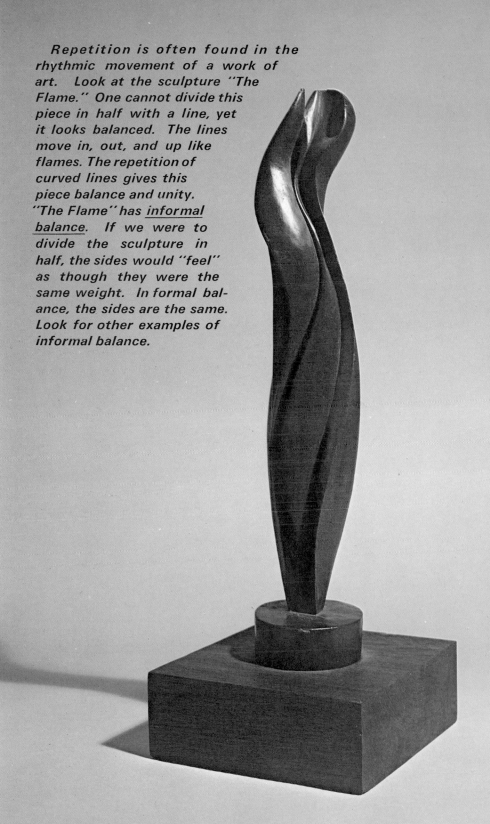

The first American locomotive was built in 1825. By 1841 the great era of the railroad had been launched.

This song tells of the plight of Pat, one of the many Irishmen who worked on a railroad crew. The job of laying and repairing track was a hard one. The men often worked in pairs, hitting alternate blows on the railroad spikes with heavy sledge hammers.

When you have learned this song, you might dramatize the movements of the railroad crew. You could also create the sounds of the hammers hitting the spikes. How many times in each measure would you expect to hear the blow of a hammer?

126

Find the phrases in this song. They are shown by
phrase lines. Which two phrases of the song are
most alike?

Pat Works on the Railway

American Railroad Song

1. In eight-een hun-dred and for-ty-one, I put me cord-'roy breech-es on,
2. In eight-een hun-dred and for-ty-two, I left the old world for the new,
3. In eight-een hun-dred and for-ty-three, 'twas then I met sweet Bid-dy Ma-gee,

I put me cord-'roy breech-es on, To work up-on the rail - way.
'I was sor-ry luck that brought me through To work up-on the rail - way.
And an el-e-gant wife she's been to me while work-in' on the rail - way.

Refrain

Fil - li - me - oo - re - i - re - ay, Fil - li - me - oo - re - i - re - ay,

Fil - li - me - oo - re - i - re - ay, To work up-on the rail - way.

Nothing is quite like a hike in the crisp morning air.
"Tiritomba" describes a morning hike in the
Italian countryside.

A tambourine would provide a good accompaniment
for this song. It could be played each time the word
"Tiritomba" is sung.

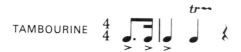

Tiritomba

Italian Folk Song

1. When the moun-tain top through pur - ple mist is glow - ing,
2. When the morn - ing dew is still to flow-ers cling - ing,

And the wood faint green is show - ing,
And the lark his song is sing - ing,

When with mer - ry rip - ple all the brooks are flow - ing,
O'er my should-er stick and bun - dle I'll be sling - ing,

Then I must be on my way.
To the road I take my way.

Refrain

Ti - ri - tom - ba,   Ti - ri - tom - ba,

{ All   the   world   is   call - ing,   call - ing   to   me   so,
{ With   my   hear - ty   song   the   coun - try - side   will   ring.

Ti - ri - tom - ba,   Ti - ri - tom - ba,   Ti - ri - tom - ba,   { I   must   go.
                                                                  { I   must   sing.

Where is repetition used to balance this song?

A prime mark (') is used to show that a repeated
phrase is changed slightly.   Which group of letters
shows the phrase form of "Tiritomba?"   Why?

A B A' B'   A A' B B'

*Look at "Berg, 1909" by Kandinsky. It
could be an illustration for the song
"Tiritomba." What colors and shapes
are repeated to give this picture balance? Does this picture have formal
balance, informal balance, or a combination of the two?*

129

Musical cadence

Each of the three sections of "Washing Day" is made of two phrases. Sing the first phrase and stop.

The_ sky with clouds was o-ver-cast, 'twas plain as plain could be,

Sing the second phrase.

It__ was no time for wash-ing clothes, as you shall sure-ly see.

Which phrase sounds unfinished?

Look at the other two sections of the song. Do the phrase endings follow the same organization as in the first section?

What effect do phrase endings have on musical balance?

The endings of phrases or sections of music are called **cadences.** Cadences that seem finished are called **full cadences.** Which of the cadences in the song "Washing Day" are full cadences?

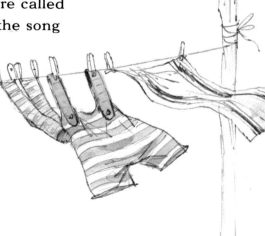

Washing Day

Scottish Reel Tune

The_ sky with clouds was o-ver-cast, 'twas plain as plain could be,
My_ Kate she is a bon-ny wife, There's none more free than she,
So_ ev-'ry morn-ing when I rise, I make a fer-vent prayer

It_ was no time for wash-ing clothes, as you shall sure-ly see.
Ex-cept up-on a wash-ing day, she acts quite dif-f'rent-ly.
Un-to the gods that it may be a wash-ing day quite fair;

My wife she frowned and as-ked me to get out of her way,
The ver-y kit-tens on the hearth dare scarce-ly ev-en play,
That gown and shirt and hand-ker-chief may end up clean and bright,

Oh, there's nar-y a bit of com-fort here Up-on a wash-ing day!
For_ fear they might get in her way Up-on a wash-ing day!
That_ we may all ex-pe-ri-ence a peace-ful day and night.

For it's thump! thump! scrub! scrub! wash! wash a-way!

There's nar-y a bit of com-fort here Up-on a wash-ing day!

John Marin painted the city as a busy, active place in "Region of Brooklyn Bridge Fantasy." There is much repetition in this painting. What components of art are repeated? Remember that the components of art are line, color, shape, value, and texture.

Make a picture about your town or city. If your town is a small, quiet one, you may want your picture to have formal balance. Formal balance is more quiet. Informal balance communicates action. Repeat some components to give balance and unity to your picture.

132

It is easy to accompany this song with autoharp or
guitar. Listen for the chord changes. Start with the
G major chord. Where do you think the harmony should
change to D7? Find the chord changes for the whole
song, playing only G major and D7.

Where are the full cadences in this song?

The Painted Bird

(Pájara Pinta)

Latin American Folk Song
Translated by Roberta McLaughlin and Bessie Stanfield

She perched in the green lem-on tree, the bird with col-ors so love-ly to see,___
Y es - ta - ba la pá - jar - a pin - ta sen - ta-da en su ver-de li - món,_

With her bright yel-low bill,___ she pecked and pecked the leaves of the green lem on tree._
Con el pi - co re -co-ge las flor - - es, Con el pi - co re - co - ge el a - mor._

Ay, ay, ay, ay!_____ The flow-ers are fair to see,___
Ay, ay, ay, ay!_____ En don - de la en-cuen - tro yo, ___

But none of them can___ com-pare With the bird in the green lem-on tree.___
Con el pi - co re - co-ge las flor - es, Con el pi - co re - co-ge el - a - mor._

Find a brace that tells you two staffs of music
are to be sung together. At this point in the song, is the
harmony part on the upper staff or on the lower staff?

At the Gate of Heaven

Spanish Folk Tune

At   the   gate   of   heav'n   lit - tle   shoes   they   are   sell - ing
A   la   puer - ta   del   cie - lo   ven - den   za - pa - tos

For   the   lit - tle   bare - foot - ed   an - gels   there   dwell - ing.
Pa - ra   an - ge - li - tos   que   an - dan   des - cal - zos.

Sleep   now,   my   lit - tle   one,   Sleep   now,   my   lit - tle   one,
Duér - me - te,   ni - ño,   Duér - me - te,   ni - ño,

Lul - la - by,   Lul - la - by,
Duér - me - te,   Duér - me - te,

Sleep   now,   my   ba - by,   a - rru,   a - rru.
Duér - me - te,   ni - ño,   a - rru,   a - rru.

134

A song puzzle

Here are four phrases of a simple dance song. Play
each phrase on the bells. It may help if you count steadily
as you play. With what count will you begin each phrase?

Rearrange the four phrases to make a melody. Put
the phrases together in various ways. Decide upon an
organization that makes the melody sound balanced.

Which of the four phrases do not have full cadences?
What do you think makes a cadence seemed finished?

This is a popular French marching song. The soldier
is singing of his wish to be with his loved one.

Auprès de Ma Blonde

French Folk Song
Translation by Alan Mills

Refrain

G   D7   G   D7   G

Oh!   just to be with   you,   I'd   be hap - py eve - ry day!
Au - près de ma blon - de,   qu'il fait bon, fait bon, fait bon!

G   D7   G   D7   G   Fine

Oh!   just to be with   you,   I'd   be glad   to stay.
Au - près de ma blon - de,   qu'il fait bon res - ter.

Solo G   D7   G   C   G

All   in   my fa - ther's gar - den   the flow - ers bloom so gay,
Au jar - din de   mon pè - re   les lau - riers sont fleu - ris,

Chorus G   D7   G   C   G

All   in   my fa - ther's gar - den   the flow - ers bloom so gay!
Au jar - din de   mon pè - re   les lau - riers sont fleu - ris!

Solo E7   Am   D7   G   D.C. al Fine

And all   the birds are nest - ing   for sum - mer's on   the way.____
Tous les   oi - seaux du mon - de   s'en vont y   faire leurs nids.____

136

The phrase form of this song is somewhat unusual.
Test yourself by answering these questions.

- How many phrases are there in the song?
- What does *D.C. al Fine* mean? Did you think of this when you counted the phrases?
- Which phrases are exactly alike?
- Which phrases are almost alike? What is the difference?
- Which phrase provides the greatest contrast?
- Where is the final cadence in this song?

In the lithograph above, the line quality is repeated. How would you describe the feeling of the lithograph? The woodcut on the right also has repetition of line. How would you describe the feeling of the woodcut?

Use ink with a pen or brush to make a line drawing of yourself. Decide whether you want your drawing to look formal and rigid, or casual and relaxed. What kinds of lines would you use to give each effect?

The ostinato

An ostinato is a pattern in music that is repeated again and
again. An ostinato helps unify the music. An ostinato may
be sung or played on instruments.

Here is an ostinato for bells. Which bells will you need
to play it?

This ostinato can be played with the round "Hey, Ho!
Anybody Home?" It can be played as an introduction,
an accompaniment to the singing, and with the **coda**.
A coda is additional music played or sung as an ending.

This song seems to go around and around without ending. Sing the song with three groups. Decide how many times to sing the song. At the end, each group may repeat the first phrase as a coda until all groups have finished.

Hey, Ho! Anybody Home?

Traditional Round

1. Hey, ho! An-y-bod-y home?

2. Meat nor drink nor mon-ey have I none;

3. Still I will be mer - - - ry.____

Coda
Hey, ho! An-y-bod-y home?

The artist Maurice Prendergast repeated several different shapes and colors in the painting "Umbrellas in the Rain." This repetition gives unity to the picture. Unity is also provided by the manner in which the picture is painted. In what manner is "Umbrellas in the Rain" painted?

Men who worked on the railroads often sang about
their work. When the tracks were being repaired, the
trains had to make a detour around the work area.
"Chicka-Hanka" is a warning to the engineer of Number 3
to get his train on the right track.

The ostinato with this song sounds like the wheels of an
approaching train. A few people might sing the melody
of the song, while others sing the ostinato very softly
and rhythmically. Play the rhythm of the ostinato on
sand blocks or a notched wood block.

Chicka-Hanka

Track Laborer's Song

Num-ber three in line A - com-in' in on time

hank-a; Chick-a-hank-a, chick-a-hank-a Chick-a-hank-a, chick-a-

Cap - tain, go side - track your train._____

hank-a; Chick-a-hank-a, chick-a-hank-a, chick-a-hank-a.

Listen to Movement II from *String Quartet No. 4* and
to "Ostinatos," page 145. Discover how ostinatos are used
differently in these two compositions.

A string quartet has two violins, a viola, and a cello.
However, these instruments are played in very unusual
ways in this movement.

A **movement** in music is a complete section. This string
quartet has five movements.

Is the music of Movement II soothing or exciting?
Which instrument plays this melody?

Listen for the ostinatos that accompany the melody.
Which instrument or instruments do you hear playing
ostinatos? How do you think the instruments are played?

The score (written music) for the first seven measures
of Movement II of *String Quartet No. 4* is on the opposite
page. The second violin and the viola play ostinatos by
tapping the strings with the wooden part of the bow.
This is called *col legno.*

The cellist plays a sustained tone by bowing. At the
same time he plays an ostinato by plucking another string.

Movement II

Andante con moto (♩ = 90)

The island of Bali is in the Indian Ocean. Balinese music often has melody patterns that sound like ostinatos. These are combined and played on instruments such as those shown below.

The Balinese orchestra is called a **gamelan.**

Ostinatos from TABUH-TABUHAN
Colin McPhee

Colin McPhee's *Tabuh-Tabuhan* sounds much like gamelan music. How many ostinatos can you hear in this piece? How do they differ from each other?

Here are three ostinatos that open the composition. What pitches are used in the first ostinato? What pitches are used in the bottom ostinato?

FLUTE, CLARINET

PIANO I

PIANO II AND MARIMBA

LISTENING *Bumblebees Sip Honey*
Balinese Dance Music

Now listen to some gamelan music from Bali. It is dance music called "Bumblebees Sip Honey." Gongs, cymbals, a pair of drums, and a xylophone-like instrument produce this music.

After you have listened, experiment with ostinatos that use two, three, four, or five tones.

MAKING MUSIC WITH OSTINATOS

1. Create some music using rhythm ostinatos. Start with three people. Each person in the trio should:

   • Choose a percussion instrument.

   • Experiment with different rhythm patterns.

   • Decide upon one pattern to play as an ostinato, and then practice it.

   Put the three patterns together. Discuss how you might begin and end the composition to make it sound balanced.

2. Develop a piece of music using tuned instruments. Organize one or more quartets. Each person in a quartet should:

   • Choose two or three resonator bells, or two or three pitches on any tuned instrument.

   • Create an ostinato and practice it.

   Combine the four ostinatos. Each person should plan to be silent at some time during the music. Discuss the effect of the rests on the composition.

3. Create a pentatonic composition that uses only ostinatos. A **pentatonic scale** has five tones. Choose a pentatonic scale that can be played on instruments in your classroom. (Examples: D E F♯A B, or E F♯G B C) You may use the pitches of your pentatonic scale in any octave.

Select a meter, such as $\frac{4}{4}$, $\frac{5}{4}$, or $\frac{3}{4}$.

Develop three or four ostinatos. Give each ostinato a different rhythm, but make the patterns simple.

Play the ostinatos together, keeping the tempo steady.

Decide upon an organization of dynamics for your composition. This might be

———◁ ▷——— or ——◁ ▷—— ◁ ▷

Decide how to begin and end your composition. Give your work a title, and perform it.

"Flags on the Pavilion," by Paul Klee, has a dark background with light lines over it. The colors in the background are blended. The light lines seem to be the same color as the background. You can make a similar effect through the technique of crayon etching. Cover a colored background with a black or dark-colored crayon. Using a compass point or pin, scratch a drawing in the crayon. This will remove the dark crayon covering and allow the background color to show through. You can create many interesting effects with this technique.

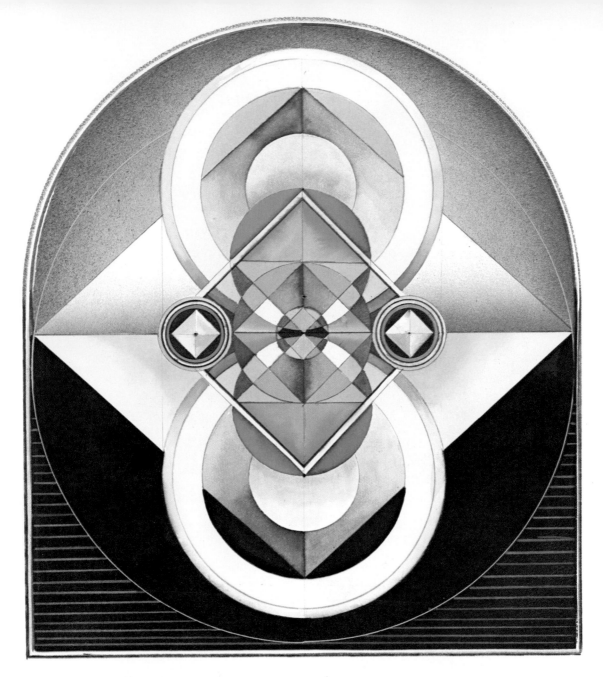

Variation in music

Some repetition is necessary to hold a piece of music together, or unify it. But too much repetition can be dull. Change is needed to make the music interesting.

Play this melody. How would you describe it?

This is the first part of "America."

There is repetition of rhythm, which provides unity.

At the same time, there is variation in pitch to create interest.

Then there is contrast of both rhythm and pitch.

Variety is also important in art. Too much repetition makes a picture dull and uninteresting. Some contrast is needed to avoid monotony. Artists can provide contrast by changing the color, line, or texture of a picture.

Melodic variation

A melody may be varied by repeating a pattern or
a phrase at different pitches. This is called **sequence**.
Where is the sequence in the melody of "Buffalo Gals"?

Buffalo Gals

American Folk Song

1. As   I   was wan-d'ring down the street, down the street, down the street,
2. I   stopped her and   I   had some talk, had some talk, had some talk,
3. She's the pret-ti-est gal I've   seen in my life, seen in my life, seen in my life,

A   pret - ty   girl   I   chanced to   meet, oh,   she was   fair   to   view.
Her foot cover-ed up   the   whole side - walk, and   left   no   room for   me.
I   wish that   she could be   my   wife, Then   we would part no   more.

Refrain

Then Buf-fa-lo gals, will you come out to-night, will you come out   to-night,

will you come out to-night, Then Buf-fa-lo   gals, will you come out   to-night,

And   dance   by   the   light   of   the   moon?

Sing this descant with the refrain.

Descant

Then Buf-fa - lo gals come out, Then Buf-fa - lo gals come out,

Then Buf-fa - lo gals come out, And dance all night.

What is the first melody pattern in "Buffalo Gals"
that is repeated in sequence?

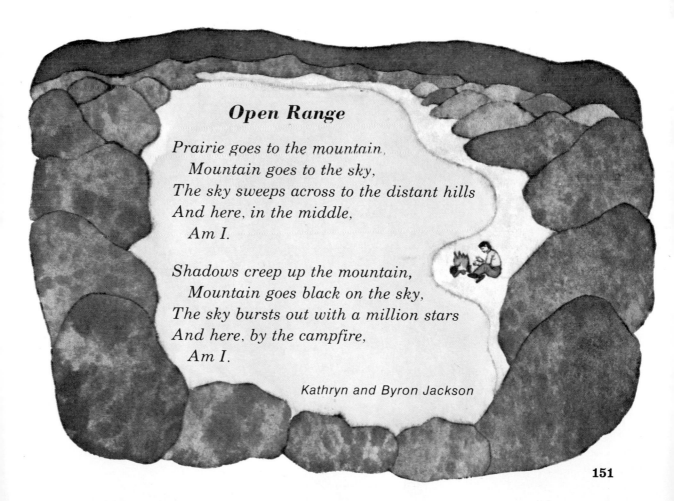

Open Range

Prairie goes to the mountain,
Mountain goes to the sky,
The sky sweeps across to the distant hills
And here, in the middle,
Am I.

Shadows creep up the mountain,
Mountain goes black on the sky,
The sky bursts out with a million stars
And here, by the campfire,
Am I.

Kathryn and Byron Jackson

My Home's in Montana

Cowboy Song
Words adapted

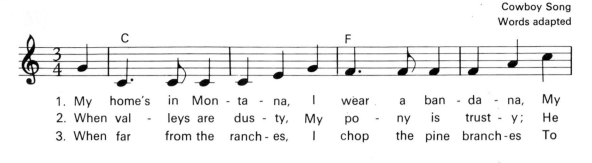

1. My home's in Mon - ta - na, I wear a ban - da - na, My
2. When val - leys are dus - ty, My po - ny is trust - y; He
3. When far from the ranch - es, I chop the pine branch - es To

spurs are of sil - ver, My po - ny is gray. When
lopes through the bliz - zard, The snow in his ears. The
heap on my camp - fire As day - light grows pale; when

rid - ing the ran - ges My luck nev - er chan - ges: With
cat - tle may scat - ter, But what does it mat - ter! My
I have par - tak - en of beans and of ba - con, I

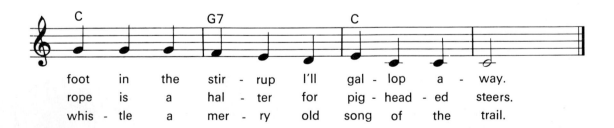

foot in the stir - rup I'll gal - lop a - way.
rope is a hal - ter for pig - head - ed steers.
whis - tle a mer - ry old song of the trail.

Where do you find sequence in this song? How does
this sequence differ from that in "Buffalo Gals"?

"Brass Band" by John Covert was made by glueing pieces of heavy cord to a background. A picture that is made of only one material could be monotonous, yet this picture is interesting. In what ways did the artist vary the cord to achieve visual interest?

Plan a string or cord picture. What can you do to make your picture interesting? When your plan is completed, dip the strings in white paste and fasten them to a cardboard background. This idea can also be used with popsicle or lollipop sticks.

Sequence is only one way of creating melodic variation. Variation may be created in other ways as well:

1. By moving some pitches up or down an octave. This is called **octave displacement.**
2. By using accidentals in unexpected places. These are called **altered tones.**
3. By adding extra notes. This is called **ornamentation.**

Here is the first phrase of the song "Streets of Laredo," page 300. Three kinds of melodic variation are shown. Play these variations on the bells. Sing the variation that uses ornamentation. Which variation do you like best?

Original version

Octave displacement

Altered tones

Ornamentation

As I_____ walked out in the streets__of La - re - do

Afro-Chinese Minuet
Harry Partch

Although the title of this composition is "Afro-Chinese Minuet," you will soon realize that it is neither African nor Chinese, nor is it a minuet. It is an altered version of a very familiar tune.

Listen to discover the name of the familar melody, and how the pitches have been changed.

LISTENING *Greeting Prelude*
Igor Stravinsky

In what ways is "Greeting Prelude" like "Afro-Chinese Minuet"? In what ways is it different?

William College Museum of Art, Photography by Sandak, Inc., N.Y.

In "Trees and Barns, Bermuda," the artist used strong contrasts in line quality to create variety and interest. The lines of the barns are straight and the edges sharp, while the lines of the tree are curved. Do you think the tree would be as interesting if the background contained similar trees?

Make a drawing in which you use two different line qualities to create contrast.

155

I Ride an Old Paint

Cowboy Song

1. I ride an old Paint, I lead an old Dan,
2. Oh, when I die, take my sad - dle from the wall,

I'm goin' to Mon - tan - a to throw the hou - li - han,
And put it on my pon - y, lead him out of his stall.

They feed in the cou - lees, they wa - ter in the draw,
Tie my bones to his back, turn our fac - es to the west,

Their tails are all mat - ted, their backs are all raw.
And we'll ride the prai - rie that we love the best.

Refrain

Ride a - round lit - tle do - gies, Ride a - round them slow,

For they're fier - y and snuf - fy and a rar - in' to go.

156

Cattle from THE PLOW THAT BROKE THE PLAINS
Virgil Thomson

What cowboy tunes do you hear in this music?
Which tune has been varied most by the composer?

List the tunes in the order they are heard. Call the
first tune A, the second B, and the third C. What is
the form of this composition?

Collection, Whitney Museum of American Art, N.Y.

Several types of variation were used in "Architectural Cadences." The buildings in the foreground are dark and strong in color. Those in the background are light and weak in color. The shapes are repeated, but the character of each is changed by its color. Find other types of variation in this picture.

Rhythmic variation

"The Tambourine" comes from Galicia, a province in the northwest corner of Spain. It is an exciting dance song with an interesting rhythm. The meter is $\frac{5}{4}$. Play this rhythm on the tambourine.

How many times can you find this rhythm pattern repeated in the melody of the song?

Play the rhythm pattern above on a tambourine at the end of each phrase.

What is the function of repetition in the song?

A repeated rhythm pattern may become monotonous. A slight variation in the pattern may create interest.

Where do you find variation of the rhythm pattern of the song?

The Tambourine

Spanish Folk Song

1. Hear this tam-bou-rine I'm play - ing, It can talk as well as play_____
2. Now this tam-bou-rine I'm play - ing Does not want to talk to - day_____

Tambourine:

It can talk as well as play_____
Does not want to talk to - day_____

With its mu - sic now is say - ing, Dance, young peo - ple, and be gay_____
For the fair - est of all maid - ens From the dance has stayed a - way_____

Tambourine:

Dance young peo - ple and be gay_____
From the dance has stayed a - way_____

Refrain

Ai - la - la - la, ai - la - la - la, Ai - la - la, la - la,

Tambourine:

Ai - la - la - la, ai - la - la - la._____

When Johnny Comes Marching Home

Words and music by Louis Lambert
Arranged by M. V. M.

LISTENING

American Salute
Morton Gould

The word **augmentation** means making longer.

What song do you hear in "American Salute?"

Where do you hear augmentation?

In this arrangement of "When the Saints Go
Marching In," one part uses augmentation. Find the
part of this song that has been augmented.

When the Saints Go Marching In

Spiritual
Arranged by M. V. M.

Oh, when the saints___ go march-ing in, ___ Oh, when the

saints go march - ing in, ___ Oh, yes, I want to

be in that num-ber, ___ when the saints go march-ing in. ___

When the saints go march-ing in, Hal - le - lu - ia,

Oh, when the saints___ go march-ing

I Hear America Singing

I hear America singing, the varied carols I hear,
Those of mechanics, each one singing his as it should be,
  blithe and strong,
The carpenter singing his as he measures his plank
  or beam,
The mason singing his as he makes ready for work,
  or leaves off work,
The boatman singing what belongs to him in his boat,
  the deck-hand singing on the steamboat deck,
The shoemaker singing as he sits on his bench,
  the hatter singing as he stands,
The woodcutter's song, the plowboy's on his way in the
  morning, or at noon intermission or at sundown,
The delicious singing of the mother, or of the young wife
  at work, or of the girl sewing or washing,
Each singing what belongs to him or her and to none else,
The day what belongs to the day—at night the party of
  young fellows, robust, friendly,
Singing with open mouths their strong melodious songs.

Walt Whitman

America

Music by Henry Carey
Words by Samuel F. Smith

1. My coun - try, 'tis of thee, Sweet land of
2. My na - tive coun - try thee, Land of the
3. Let mu - sic swell the breeze, And ring from
4. Our fa - thers' God, to Thee, Au - thor of

lib - er - ty, Of thee I sing.
no - ble free, Thy name I love.
all the trees Sweet Free - dom's song;
lib - er - ty, To Thee we sing.

Land where my fa - thers died! Land of the pil - grims' pride!
I love thy rocks and rills, Thy woods and tem - pled hills;
Let mor - tal tongues a - wake, Let all that breathe par - take,
Long may our land be bright With Free - dom's ho - ly light;

From ev - 'ry__ moun - tain side, Let __ free - dom ring!
My heart_ with__ rap - ture thrills Like__ that a - bove.
Let rocks_ their__ si - lence break, The __ sound pro - long.
Pro - tect__ us __ by Thy might, Great God, our King!

Creating musical variations

What variations could you create for "America"? Here
are a few ideas. Sing or play "America" with the
variations below. Then try to think of others.

My coun-try 'tis of thee, Sweet land of lib - er-ty, Of thee I sing!

My coun-try 'tis of thee, Sweet land of lib - er-ty, Of thee I sing!

My coun-try 'tis_ of_ thee, Sweet land of lib- er-ty, Of thee I sing.

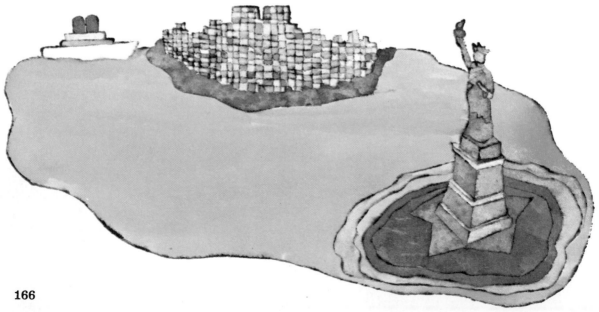

Charles Ives wrote this music for the organ in 1891.
In 1963 another composer, William Schuman, arranged it
for orchestra. This entire composition was built by creating
variations on the melody of "America." The form of the
composition is called **theme and variations,** or simply
variation form.

The first time you listen to this music, try to find a
variation like one of those you sang or played. What other
kinds of variation can you hear in this composition?

Charles Ives, composer of the original organ variations,
was the son of a band leader in the Civil War. At the
age of 12, he played the drums in his father's band.
Charles studied piano and organ with his father and soon
began to compose music. Throughout his life he
experimented with musical ideas. He tried daring new
harmonies, textures, rhythms, scales, and combinations
of instruments. He often wove into his music the folk
tunes, hymn tunes, and patriotic music of America.
Although Ives' music reflected American life, it was not
recognized as great until near the end of the composer's
life. Ives died in 1954 at the age of 80. Today he is
regarded as a pioneer in modern music, and as a composer
who used musical ideas far ahead of his time.

© Clara Aich

CAREERS

Organists can play both pipe and electronic organs. Pipe organs are found in churches, concert halls, and theaters. Electronic organs are usually found in homes, churches, restaurants, and sports stadiums. Organists are in demand for religious services, weddings, and concerts.

Life Styles: Two Variations

(1)

My home's in Montana,
I wear a bandanna,
My spurs are of silver,
My pony is gray.
When riding the ranges,
My luck never changes,
With foot in the stirrup,
I'll gallop away.

—Cowhand's song

(2)

My home's near the city,
My ties really fit me,
My shoes are of leather,
My auto is brown.
When driving the highways,
I pass all the byways,
With foot on the pedal,
I'll hurry to town.

—Commuter's song

Often an artist will choose a subject and paint it in several different ways. Look at these drawings of the same flower. How do they differ?

Use an idea from the poems on life styles and paint a picture. Then paint several variations of your picture.

Music and dance

Dancing is more than movement.

Dancing is a means of expressing feelings.

Dancing is a form of entertainment.

Dancing is a social experience.

Dancing is an art.

Nearly all dancing is done to music.

Music and dance belong together.

The Ballerina and the Moor then begin to waltz. Petrouchka rushes in, but the Moor pushes him out the door.

The carnival is the setting once again as Scene 4 opens. A group of nursemaids enter and dance. Next a peasant arrives, leading a bear. The bear walks on his hind legs while the peasant plays a pipe.

Dance of the Nursemaids

(*heard an octave lower*)

Others enter, and soon the stage is filled with dancers. Suddenly a cry is heard! Petrouchka, followed by the Moor, rushes out of the puppet theater. The Moor strikes Petrouchka who falls, lifeless.

The Showman assures the crowd that Petrouchka was only a stuffed puppet. As he begins to drag Petrouchka toward the little theater, he looks up and sees the ghost of Petrouchka rising above the booths. Terrified, the Showman drops Petrouchka and runs away.

As you listen many times to the music from *Petrouchka,* think about how Stravinsky expressed the story.

> For what purpose did the composer use the Russian folk tune, "Down the Peterskaya Road"?
>
> What instruments play the "Dance of the Ballerina"? What do they tell you about the dancer?
>
> How does the music tell you when the bear begins to dance?
>
> What instrument plays the first solo in the "Bear Dance"? Why do you think Stravinsky chose this instrument?
>
> Does the ballet music end softly or loudly? Why?
>
> Does the music from *Petrouchka* make you want to dance? Why?

Music, drama, and dance: The opera

An **opera** is a drama told through acting, singing, and instrumental music. The dialogue (conversation) in an opera is usually sung. In most operas an orchestra accompanies the singers. Sometimes there is music for the orchestra alone. Dancing is also an important part of many operas.

Operas are usually staged. A staged production includes costumes, scenery, and lighting. In order to perform in an opera, a person must be able to sing and act well.

Two people may be involved in writing an opera. One is the **librettist,** the person who writes the **libretto** (the words of the story). The other person is the composer of the music. Many changes may be necessary in both the libretto and the music before they fit together.

Operas have been written and performed for almost four hundred years. *Amahl and the Night Visitors* is a one-act opera that was written not long ago. Gian-Carlo Menotti wrote both the words and the music for this opera.

Amahl and the Night Visitors was the first opera to be written especially for television. It was first presented on Christmas Eve, 1951. For many years it has been a feature on television at Christmas time.

A short version of *Amahl and the Night Visitors* is presented here for you to read and sing. The entire class may sing the songs. After you have sung and listened to the music, you may wish to perform it as a musical play. When this is done, a reader will not be needed.

Amahl and the Night Visitors

by Gian-Carlo Menotti

CAST OF CHARACTERS

Amahl, a crippled boy of about 12

Amahl's mother

King Kaspar

King Melchior

King Balthazar

A Page

A group of shepherds

SETTING: The shepherd's hut where Amahl and his mother live.

The opera opens with a short overture.   An overture is an instrumental introduction.   After the overture, Amahl's pipe is heard. *(Recording: "Overture")*

READER

It is night. The sky is clear and filled with stars. Amahl, a poor, lame shepherd boy, is sitting outside his hut looking at the sky and playing his shepherd's pipe.

MOTHER

(From inside the house) Amahl! Amahl! Time to go to bed.

AMAHL

Coming.

READER

After a moment, Amahl begins to play his pipe again.

MOTHER

How long must I shout to make you obey?

AMAHL

I'm sorry, Mother, but—let me stay a little longer. The sky is still light, and the moon hasn't risen yet.

MOTHER
  There won't be any moon tonight, but there
  will be a weeping child very soon, if he doesn't
  obey his mother.

AMAHL
  Oh, very well.

READER
  Amahl picks up his crutch and hobbles into the house.
  He hangs up his cloak and cap, then goes to the
  door again and looks up at the sky.

MOTHER
  What was keeping you outside?

AMAHL
  Oh, Mother, you should go out and see. There's
  never been such a sky. Hanging over our roof there
  is a star as large as a window, and the star has a tail,
  and it moves across the sky like a chariot on fire.

185

BALTHAZAR

May we rest a while in your house and warm
ourselves by your fireplace?

MOTHER

I am a poor widow, but you are welcome to all I have.

KASPAR

Oh,　thank　you,　thank　you,　thank　you!

READER

A Page enters the hut first, and puts his lantern down.
Then the three kings march in, Kasper first, Balthazar
next, and Melchior third. Each king carries a gift.
The Page holds the train of each king as he enters.
He then puts a rug in front of them and places the
gifts on the rug. *(Recording: "March of the Kings")*

MOTHER

I shall go and gather wood for the fire. I shall be
right back. Amahl, don't be a bother.

AMAHL

No, Mother.

READER

As soon as Amahl's mother leaves, Amahl begins
to ask the kings all kinds of questions.

AMAHL

(to Balthazar) Are you a *real* King?

BALTHAZAR

Yes.

AMAHL

Have you royal blood?

BALTHAZAR

Yes.

AMAHL

Can I see it?

BALTHAZAR

It is just like yours.

AMAHL

What's the use of having it, then?

BALTHAZAR

No use. And you, little boy, what do you do?

AMAHL

Sadly

I was a shep - herd, I had a flock of sheep.

But my Moth-er sold them, sold them. Now there are no sheep left.

I had a black goat who gave me warm sweet milk. But she died of old age,

old age. Now there is no goat left. But

Moth - er says that now we shall both go

beg - ging from door to door. Won't it be fun?

BALTHAZAR

It has its points.

AMAHL

(Pointing to Kaspar's jeweled box) And what is this?

KASPAR

This is my box, this is my box, I nev-er trav-el with-out my box.

READER

Kaspar shows Amahl beads and jewels from the box,
and gives him some candy. As Amahl is eating it,
his mother returns.

MOTHER

Amahl, go and call the other shepherds. Tell them
about our visitors, and ask them to bring whatever
they have, for we have nothing.

READER

Amahl grabs his cloak and hat, and hurries out to tell
the other shepherds. The mother carries the wood
to the fireplace. As she is putting it down, she notices
the gold, incense, and myrrh.

MOTHER

Oh, these beautiful things, and *all that gold!*

MELCHIOR

These are the gifts for the Child. We don't know Him,
but the Star will guide us to Him.

MOTHER

What does the Child look like?

MELCHIOR

Have you seen a Child the col-or of wheat, the col-or of dawn? His

eyes are mild, His hands are those of a King, as King He was born.

In - cense, myrrh, and gold we bring to His side,

and the East - ern Star is our guide.

MOTHER

Yes, I know a child the col-or of wheat, the col-or of dawn. His

eyes are mild, His hands are those of a King, as King he was born.

But no one will bring him in-cense or gold, though sick and

poor and hun-gry and cold. He's my child, my son, my dar-ling, my own.

MELCHIOR

The Child we seek holds the seas and the winds on his palm.

KASPAR

The Child we seek has the moon and the stars at his feet.

BALTHAZAR

Before Him the eagle is gentle, the lion is meek.

THREE KINGS

Choirs of angels hover over his roof and sing Him to sleep.

(Pause)

MOTHER

Listen, the shepherds are coming.

READER

The shepherds arrive, first one by one, then in twos
and threes, led by Amahl. They are carrying baskets
of fruit and vegetables, and they are singing.

SHEPHERDS

1. Em - i - ly, Em - i - ly, Mi - chael, Bar - thol - o - mew,
2. Ben - ja - min, Ben - ja - min, Lu - cas, E - liz - a - beth,
3. Kath - er - ine, Kath - er - ine, Chris - to - pher, Ba - bi - la

how are your chil - dren and how are your sheep?
how are your chil - dren and how are your sheep?
how are your chil - dren and how are your sheep?

Dor - o - thy, Dor - o - thy, Pe - ter, E - van - ge - line,
Car - o - lyn, Car - o - lyn, Mat - thew, Ver - on - i - ca,
Jo - seph-ine, Jo - seph-ine, An - ge - la, Jer - e - my,

1,2 give me your hand, come a - long with me.
give me your hand, come a - long with me.
3 come _____ a - long with me.

196

READER

The shepherds crowd at the door of the hut to see the kings, but they are afraid to enter. Finally, one by one, they slip in and offer their gifts to the royal visitors.

KINGS

Thank you, thank you, thank you kind-ly. Thank you, thank you, thank you kind-ly too.

MOTHER

Now won't you dance for them?

READER

The shepherds are very shy at first. Then an old shepherd and Amahl begin to play their pipes, and gradually the men and women join in the dancing. *(Recording: "Dance of the Shepherds")*

BALTHAZAR

Thank you, good friends, for your dances and your gifts. Now we must bid you good night.

READER

The shepherds bow to the kings as they leave. Amahl, his mother, and the kings say goodnight to each other and prepare to sleep. But Amahl's mother cannot take her eyes from the gold, which the Page is guarding.

MOTHER

All that gold! All that gold! I wonder if rich people know what to do with their gold! Oh, what I could do for my child with that gold. If I take some, they'll never miss it . . . *(Recording: "All That Gold")*

READER

The Mother slowly crosses the room. As she touches
the gold, the Page grabs her arm.

PAGE

Thief! Thief! I saw her steal some of the gold!

READER

Amahl awakens and sees the Page holding his mother.
He rushes to him, and begins to hit the Page and
pull his hair.

AMAHL

Don't you dare hurt my mother. Oh, Mister King,
don't let him hurt my mother.

MELCHIOR

Woman, you may keep the gold. The Child we seek doesn't need our gold. He will someday be a King who will rule with love.

MOTHER

Take back your gold. If I weren't so poor I would send a gift of my own to such a King.

AMAHL

But mother, let me send Him my crutch. He may need one, and this I made myself.

READER

As Amahl lifts his crutch to hand it to the kings, he takes a step. Suddenly, he realizes he can walk.

KINGS AND MOTHER

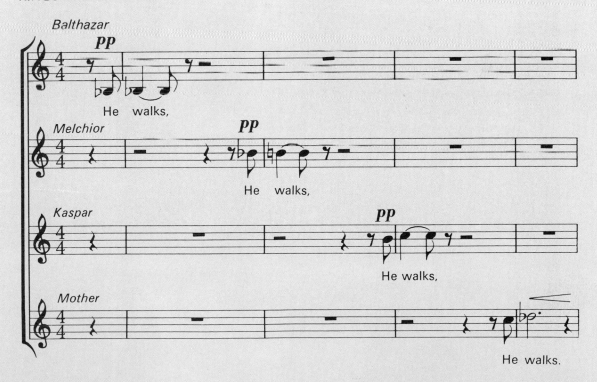

Look, Moth-er, I can dance, I can jump, I can run!

KINGS

Tru - ly, he can dance, he can jump, he___ can___ run!

200

AMAHL

Oh, Mother, let me go with the kings. I want to take the crutch to the Child myself.

KINGS

Let him come with us.

MOTHER

Yes, I think you should go and bring thanks to the Child yourself.

READER

The Page leads the kings from the hut. As Amahl joins the procession, he begins to play his pipe. The soft colors of dawn are filling the sky, and a few large flakes of snow have begun to fall upon the road. *(Recording: "Amahl's Pipe Music")*

The perspectives of music

Music has many functions in people's lives. Music can often express feelings and ideas better than words. Music can create appropriate moods for important events.

Music can help us understand other times and places. It can also help us understand the world in which we live today.

Artists are influenced by everything that they can see or think about. The sources for their ideas include activities of everyday life, nature, dreams and fantasy, religious beliefs, and political and historical events.

What makes music "popular"?

In the following pages, you will have a chance to hear and sing many types of music that have been called "popular." Styles in popular music change from year to year, just as other styles change. Popular music expresses the time and place from which it comes.

One type of popular music is rock. The media of rock—voices, electric guitars, electronic organs, and drums—express a particular mood as no other media can. As you hear and sing "Changing," think about the words. What do they say about the world in which you live?

Changing

Music by Bill Brohn
Words by George Guilbault

Where does popular music come from?

Many of the songs that you hear on the radio or on television first appeared in a musical play or a movie.

Look at these photographs. They may remind you of popular songs you know.

" The Sound of Music"

"The Wizard of Oz"

"Mary Poppins"

"Happiness" from
You're a Good Man, Charlie Brown
Clark Gesner

"Happiness" is a song from the musical play *You're a Good Man, Charlie Brown.* This show is based on the popular comic strip "Peanuts" by Charles Schulz.

What do the words of the song tell you *happiness* is?

"You're a Good Man, Charlie Brown"

TO THOSE OF US WITH REAL UNDERSTANDING, DANCING IS THE ONLY PURE ART FORM!

© 1963 United Feature Syndicate, Inc.

207

"It's a Small World" was first introduced at a World's Fair. If you have been to Disneyland, you may have heard it at the exhibit "It's a Small World."

It's a Small World

Words and music by Richard M. Sherman
and Robert B. Sherman
Arranged by C. A. R.

Descant

1. It's a world of laugh - ter, world of tears;
2. There is just one moon, one gol - den sun;

Melody G   D7

1. It's a world of laugh - ter, a world of tears; it's a
2. There is just one moon and one gol - den sun and a

it's a world of hopes, a world of fears.   There's so
and a smile means friend - ship, ev - 'ry - one.   Though the

G

world of hopes and a world of fears. There's so much that we
smile means friend - ship to ev - 'ry - one. Though the moun - tains di -

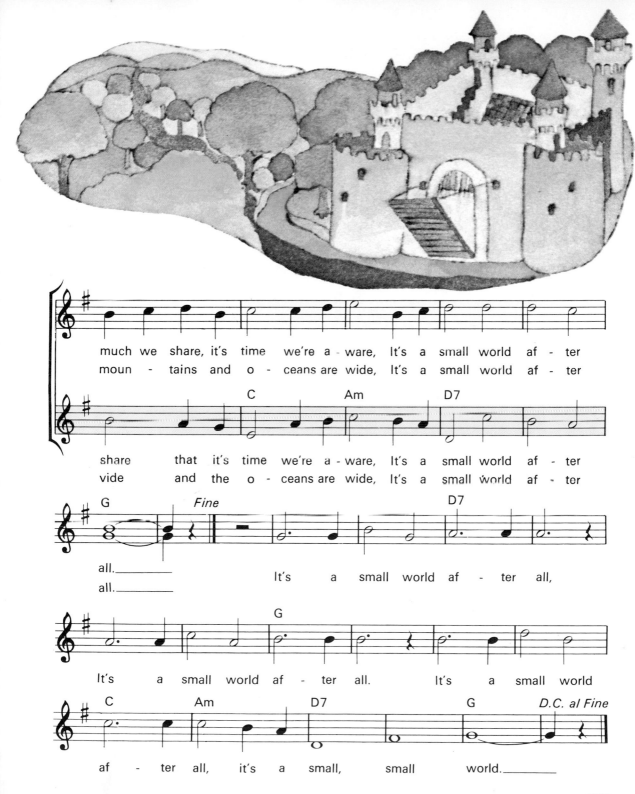

much we share, it's time we're a - ware, It's a small world af - ter
moun - tains and o - ceans are wide, It's a small world af - ter

C   Am   D7

share   that it's time we're a - ware, It's a small world af - ter
vide   and the o - ceans are wide, It's a small world af - ter

G   *Fine*   D7

all._____   It's a small world af - ter all,
all._____

G

It's a small world af - ter all.   It's a small world

C   Am   D7   G   *D.C. al Fine*

af - ter all, it's a small, small world._____

Some artists of today make paintings and sculptures of things that people see every day. These things are part of what is called popular culture.

How would you make such a work of art? What media could you use? This picture could help you answer these questions. The work of art you see here is an example of *pop art*.

210

Bizet Has His Day
Les Brown

Les Brown used the folk melody "March of the Three Kings" as the theme for a composition. You may remember that Bizet used the same melody in his *L'Arlésienne Suite No. 1,* page 47. Listen to Bizet's work again. Then listen to Les Brown's. After you have heard both pieces, ask yourself these questions.

1. How is Les Brown's music different from Bizet's?
2. In what ways is Les Brown's music different from the music of today?
3. What unusual sounds does Les Brown use at the beginning and near the end of the composition?
4. What instruments do you hear in Les Brown's composition?

St. Louis Blues
W. C. Handy

W. C. Handy was a black musician. He began writing music around the turn of the century. When Handy was a boy, he bought a trumpet for a dollar and taught himself to play it. Later, he ran away from home to join a show. He eventually became a band leader. As he toured the country with his band, he helped make music known as the **blues** become popular.

"St. Louis Blues" is one of the best known of W. C. Handy's compositions. As you listen to it, ask yourself the following questions.

1. How would you describe the mood of this music?
2. Are all of the phrases of the same length, or of different lengths?
3. Why do you think this type of music is called "blues"?

Keeping a record of popular songs

What songs are popular at this time? What makes a song interesting to you? Is it the words, the melody, the rhythm, the performers, or the combination of instruments?

Some radio stations and record stores feature the most popular songs of each week. Make a list of the most popular songs each week in your town. Find out how long they remain on the list of the top five or ten recordings. Discuss in class what you think makes a song popular.

Find out where the song was first introduced. Was it on a recording by a popular performing group, on a television program, in a movie or a musical?

List the instruments and the kinds of voices you hear in the recording.

Do recordings of certain performers appear frequently near the top of the list? If so, why do you think those performers are so popular?

TITLE	PERFORMING GROUP	WHEN FIRST APPEARED

The music of early America

History books can tell you about events of the past.
History books can tell you how people felt about the
events that took place during their lifetime.

Music and art can also help us understand the past.
They help us understand in a very different way. As
you explore the music in the following pages, try to
imagine the feelings of the people who created the works.
Find a way of expressing those feelings as you listen to
or perform the music. Choose tempos and dynamics that
best express the mood of each song.

Traveling shows were presented by groups of singers and dancers during the second half of the nineteenth century. Many songs from these shows are still sung today.

Dan Emmett was one of the most famous composers of songs for these traveling shows. When Dan was a boy, he was a piper in an Army band, then a drummer in a circus. Finally he became a performer in a show. He enjoyed his work so much that he began writing songs for the shows. Three of his most famous songs are "Dixie," "Blue-Tailed Fly," and "Old Dan Tucker."

Old Dan Tucker

Words and music by Dan Emmett

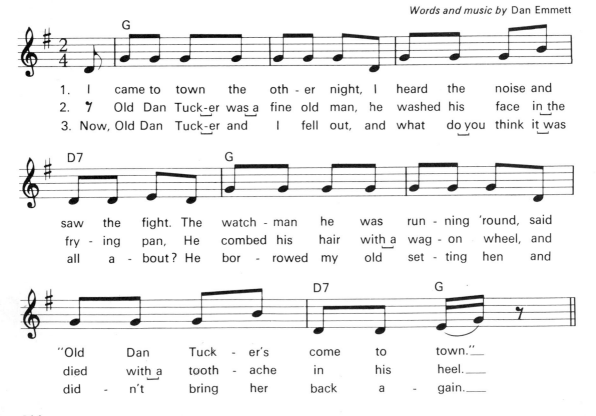

1. I came to town the oth-er night, I heard the noise and
2. Old Dan Tuck-er was a fine old man, he washed his face in the
3. Now, Old Dan Tuck-er and I fell out, and what do you think it was

saw the fight. The watch-man he was run-ning 'round, said
fry-ing pan, He combed his hair with a wag-on wheel, and
all a - bout? He bor-rowed my old set-ting hen and

"Old Dan Tuck - er's come to town."
died with a tooth - ache in his heel.
did - n't bring her back a - gain.

Refrain

C   D7   G

Get out the way, Old Dan Tuck-er, Get out the way, Old Dan Tuck-er,

C   D7   G

Get out the way, Old Dan Tuck-er, You're too late to come to sup-per.

4. Old Dan began in early life
to play the banjo and win a wife,
But every time a date he'd keep
he'd play himself right fast asleep.
Refrain

5. Now, Old Dan Tucker he came to town
to swing the ladies all around,
Swing them right and swing them left
then to the one he liked the best.
Refrain

6. And when Old Dan had passed away
they missed the music he used to play,
They took him on his final ride
and buried his banjo by his side.
Refrain

215

Come, Come, Ye Saints

Traditional melody
Words by William Clayton

1. Come, come, ye saints, no toil nor la-bor fear, But with joy
2. We'll find the place which God for us pre-pared Far a-way

wend our way. Though hard to you this jour-ney may ap-pear,
in the West, Where none shall come to hurt or make a-fraid;

Grace shall be as your day. 'Tis___ bet-ter far_____ for
There the saints will be blessed. We'll make the air_____ with

us to strive,___ Our use-less cares,___ from us to drive; Do
mu-sic ring,___ Shout prais-es to___ our God and King; A-

this, and joy your hearts will swell, All is well! All is well!
bove the rest these words we'll tell, All is well! All is well!

In May 1848, the Mormons, a religious group, set out from Missouri for a long trip west. They were short of food, and many died before the journey ended. They had little hope left. Their leader, Brigham Young, thought that a song would lift the spirits of his people. William Clayton, a member of the group, thought of some inspiring words as he walked along. That night, around the campfire, he taught "Come, Come, Ye Saints" to the others.

The group safely reached the area which became Salt Lake City, Utah. It was this kind of courage against impossible odds that opened the Western frontiers of this country. What words in this song do you think gave courage to the Mormons?

Since there were no cameras in pioneer days, scenes and people had to be drawn or painted. Many early portraits were painted by artists who traveled from town to town. These artists were often self-taught. They produced many works and often did not sign them. Look at the two pictures above. What can you learn about Colonial America from examining these works?

Because the early settlers had little more than the bare necessities, entertainment centered around simple things that people could do together. Sometimes a family gathered around a pump organ or a piano to sing.

Occasionally, at a community gathering, some of the older people would sing about something from their past that they enjoyed.

The Singing School

Traditional Round

I will sing you a song of the old Sing-ing School

and the sounds you there may___ hear;

Of the do, re, mi and the A, B, C

and the voic - es ring - ing clear.

Sing the song with ac - cent strong,

Loud and clear the tone pro - long.

3. Do, re, mi, fa, sol, la, ti, do;

'tis the scale of___ C, you know. Com - mon, dou - ble,

tri - ple, meas-ures, too, are a - mong the man - y things we do.

In many of the singing schools, "shaped notes" were used. In this system of notation, each tone of the scale had its own shape. This helped the singers identify the notes. The first part of "The Singing School" would look like this if it were written in shaped notes.

Years before the pioneers settled the West, French settlers roamed the waterways and woodlands from the Great Lakes to the Gulf of Mexico. Most of the settlers were soldiers and traders.

As they paddled up and down the rivers in their birch canoes, they sang of their adventurous life.

Voyageur's Song

French-Canadian Song

Pad - dle to - geth - er____ where the wa - ter's deep and blue;
Pad - dle to - geth - er____ when the morn - ing's cool and clear,

Pad - dle to - geth - er and sing - ing as we do.
Pad - dle to - geth - er, No man or beast we fear.

Fish is fine for break - fast when the sun comes up so cheer - ful - ly;

Oh, fish is fine for break-fast and a girl is fine to kiss.

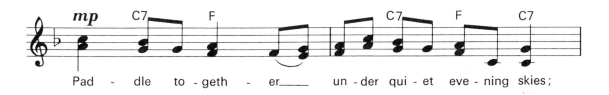

Pad - dle to - geth - er___ un - der qui - et eve - ning skies;

Pad - dle to - geth - er and if you love, be wise!

The English colonists who settled this country continued to follow customs that were familiar to them. Many songs they sang were those brought from across the seas. Thus, many of the songs and stories of early America were English in origin.

Let Simon's Beard Alone

Traditional English Song

1. Let Si - mon's beard a - lone, a-lone, __ let Si - mon's beard a - lone;__

2. 'Tis no __ dis - grace to Si - mon's face__, for he had nev - er one;__

3. Then mock not, nor scoff not, nor jeer not, nor sneer not, but

rath - er him be - moan.__

The Wraggle Taggle Gypsies

English Folk Song

1. There— were three gyp - sies a - come to my door,
2. Then— she pulled off her— silk fin - ished gown,
3. It was late last night when my lord came— home,

And down - stairs ran this - a la - dy, O!
And put on hose of— leath - er, O!
In - quir - ing for his la - dy, O!

The one sang high, and an - oth - er sang low,
The rag - ged rags a - bout— our door,
The ser - vants said on— ev - 'ry hand,

And the oth - er sang, "Bon - ny, bon - ny Bis - cay, O!"
And she's gone— with the wrag - gle - tag - gle gyp - sies, O!
She's gone— with the wrag - gle - tag - gle gyp - sies, O!

The colonies along the Eastern seacoast grew and prospered. Their mother country, England, began to tax the people. The colonists resented the high taxes on items such as tea. One night a group of colonists climbed aboard a ship anchored in the Boston harbor. They dumped a cargo of tea into the bay. The colonists must have enjoyed singing "Revolutionary Tea," a song about the Boston Tea Party.

Revolutionary Tea

Words *by* Seba Smith
Music *by* H. D. Munson

1. There was an old La - dy lived o - ver the sea, And
she was an Is - land Queen;___ Her daught-er lived off in a
new___ coun-trie, With an O - cean of wa - ter be - tween;___
The old la - dy's pock - ets were full___ of gold, But

2. "Now, Moth - er, dear Moth - er," the daught-er re - plied, "I
shan't do the thing_ you ax,_____ I'm will - ing to pay a fair
price for the tea, But___ nev - er the three-pen - ny tax;"___
"You shall," quoth the moth - er, and red - den'd with rage, "For

nev - er con -tent - ed was she:_____ So she called on her daught-er to
you're my own daught-er you see,_____ And_ sure, 'tis quite pro - per the

pay her a tax Of three pence a pound on her tea,
daught - er should pay Her moth er a tax on her tea,

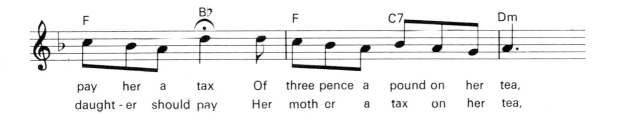

Of three pence a pound on her tea._____
Her moth - er a tax on her tea.''_____

3. And so the old lady her servant called up,
   And packed off a budget of tea,
   And eager for three pence a pound, she put in
   Enough for a large familie,
   She ordered her servants to bring home the tax,
   Declaring her child should obey,
   Or old as she was and almost woman grown,
   She'd half whip her life away,
   She'd half whip her life away.

4. The tea was conveyed to the daughter's door,
   All down by the ocean's side,
   And the bouncing girl pour'd out every pound
   In the dark and boiling tide ;
   And then she called out to the Island Queen,
   "Oh Mother, dear Mother," quoth she,
   "Your tea you may have when 'tis steep'd enough,
   But never a tax from me,
   No ! never a tax from me."

You have sung a few songs that tell how people of long ago felt and what they thought. Imagine that you are a historian living 500 years from now, and you discover a collection of songs that were popular during the 1980's. You examine the words and the musical mood of the songs, and write about your findings. What conclusion do you think you would reach? What would you think about the way the people of our time felt and what they considered to be important?

Katherine Young

Music of the European nobility

While the traders and colonists were struggling to make a home in the wilderness of America, a very different kind of life was being lived in Europe. There, many wealthy families owned huge estates. Their homes were large and luxurious. They had servants and tenant farmers who worked their land. Although the European working people had few luxuries, the nobility had many.

Entertainment was often provided by court musicians. Composers were in great demand to write music for special occasions, as well as for everyday entertainment.

The Age of Bach

If you had lived in Europe at the time of Johann
Sebastian Bach, you might have heard music that was in
some ways like the popular music of today.   Today's
music has a steady beat.   Often it is played by guitars.
Listen especially for the beat and the guitar sound as
you hear the recording of "Baroquin' Rock."
Music in the time of Bach was written in a
style called Baroque.

Baroquin' Rock

Music by Bill Brohn
Words by George Guilbault

Tin - kle a tune_ that swings in the mid - dle,

Drum out a bass where eighth notes once poured.

Come swing with it,

Come play_ with it, Bar-oqu-in' Rock_ on a harp-si - chord!

J.___ S. Bach once

grooved in the rhy - thm,

Vi - val - di was a play-er who soared.

Now, you_ can be right there with 'em, Bar-oqu-in' Rock___ on a

harp - si - chord.

Minuet II
from FRENCH SUITE NO. 1 IN D MINOR
Johann Sebastian Bach
Rock Arrangement

Bach lived and composed music in the early 1700's.
The strong beat and clear structure of Bach's music have
attracted some of the popular performing groups of today.

Listen to Bach's "Minuet II" played on the harpsichord,
electric bass, and drums. This theme is in the minuet.

How is this composition like "Baroquin' Rock"?

Alfred Fisher

LISTENING *Minuet II*
from FRENCH SUITE NO. 1 IN D MINOR
Johann Sebastian Bach

Now listen to the minuet as it might have been heard
in Bach's time. It is played on the **harpsichord.** The
harpsichord is a keyboard instrument. It looks something
like a small grand piano, but its sound is very different.
The sound of the harpsichord is produced by tiny picks.
These picks pluck the strings inside the instrument when
the keys are pressed.

In what ways does the harpsichord performance of the
minuet sound different from the version with electric
guitar, string bass, and drums?

Sonata, Allegro, March, and Battle from BATTALIA
Heinrich Biber

During the 1600's, the instruments of the violin family were perfected by a group of skilled Italian workers. The most famous of these instrument makers was Antonio Stradivari. Composers all over Europe began to write music for these new instruments. They enjoyed experimenting with various possibilities for new sounds.

Heinrich Biber was a composer and violinist who lived in Germany in the late 1600's. Biber's *Battalia,* for string orchestra, describes a battle. The work contains several movements; you will hear four of them. Decide which battle sounds the composer tried to imitate. How do the players produce these sounds on their instruments?

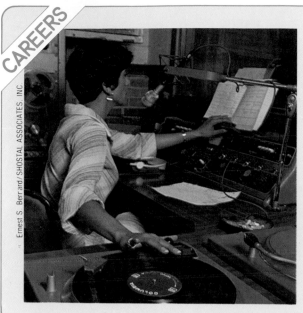

Ernest S. Berrard/SHOSTAL ASSOCIATES, INC.

A **radio announcer** may introduce classical music, commenting on the music and the composer as well as the recording itself. An announcer's style and personality should appeal to a wide audience. An announcer should speak clearly and with an expressive voice. Often the title of a musical selection is in a foreign language. A radio announcer needs to have some knowledge of how to pronounce words in many different languages.

Radio announcers must also know the kinds of music that are of interest to their listeners. Knowing about many kinds of music is important.

LISTENING *CONCERTO IN G MAJOR FOR VIOLIN AND ORCHESTRA*
First Movement Antonio Vivaldi

The perfection of stringed instruments made possible the growth of the string orchestra. Composers began to write music to display the beautiful tone and expressive power of these new instruments. One composer who wrote music for the new stringed instruments was Antonio Vivaldi. He wrote over 400 concertos for many different stringed instruments. You may remember that a concerto is a work for solo instrument (or a group of solo instruments) and orchestra. Listen to the first movement of one of Vivaldi's violin concertos.

The orchestra begins with this theme.

Listen for scale patterns in the melody, contrasts between loud sections and soft sections, and a steady rhythmic pulse. These are all typical of string music from Vivaldi's time.

233

Georg Philip Telemann was another composer who lived during the time of Bach. He was acquainted with both Bach and Handel.

As you sing Telemann's song "Good Luck," notice the contrast between the galloping rhythm of the eighth notes and the rhythm of the long dotted quarter notes.

Good Luck

Music by George Philip Telemann
Words by Ronald P. Smyth

Good luck may not come when you al - ways ex - pect it, but

when it does, you'll know it's there.

It may not ar - rive in a coach or a car - riage, but

when it does, you'll know it's there.

234

It may not sur - prise you but some-times it comes by a

po - ny rid - ing ver - y slow - ly, Gid - dy - up! Gid - dy - up!

Luck__ may come in a wag - on as it winds its

way from place to place to you.

The Age of Haydn and Mozart

In the years following the Age of Bach, music continued to change. One of the foremost composers of the new type of music was Franz Joseph Haydn, who lived about 200 years ago. During this era, the strong power of the nobility was beginning to lessen, and the middle class gained influence. Although composers were still hired by the very wealthy, a new independence was in the air.

LISTENING *QUARTET IN C MAJOR, Op. 33, No. 3 ("The Bird"), Fourth Movement*
Franz Joseph Haydn

Many of Haydn's compositions have been given nicknames. You will hear the last movement from a quartet often called "The Bird." Why do you think it was given this title? Here is the opening melody. Listen for its return several times during the movement.

Near the middle of the movement, you will hear the theme given below. How many times do you hear this theme? How would you describe the mood of this music?

This painting by Max Oppenheim is called "String Quartet." You can see all four instruments of the quartet in the painting. But the painter was more interested in conveying a feeling for the music than in showing the quartet in a realistic way. From the arrangement of objects in the painting and the colors used can you tell what kind of music the quartet is playing? Is it slow or fast? Gentle or agitated? Gay or mournful?

Optimism and love of life were expressed in Haydn's music. "The Heavens Resound" is a joyful song of praise.

The Heavens Resound

Music by Joseph Haydn from *The Creation*
Words by Andreas Hofer

The Heav - ens re - sound with His prais - es e - ter - nal,

In___ might___ and___ glo - ry they___ com - bine___

To tell His name through earth___ and___ o - ceans,

That_ man___ may___ hear the word___ di - vine.

He holds the suns in the blue vault-ed heav-ens,

He lifts_____ the moun - - tains of_____ the world;

The count - less stars bow in will - ing sub - jec - tion;

The u - - ni - verse_____ His hand un - furled.

239

Another famous composer of the late 1700's was
Wolfgang Amadeus Mozart. He was born after Haydn
and was one of the most gifted composers that ever lived.
He wrote many symphonies, string quartets, operas, and
much piano music.

"Papageno's Song" is from Mozart's opera,
The Magic Flute. Papageno is a bird catcher by
profession and dresses in feathers. He sings this song
to introduce himself in the opera.

Papageno's Song

Music by Wolfgang A. Mozart
Words Adapted

1. I___ am a sim - ple,_ qui - et man, I___ play up - on my pipes of Pan.
2. I___ am a sim - ple,_ qui - et man, I___ play up - on my pipes of Pan.

Of catch - ing_ birds I___ make a game, And Pa - pa-ge - no is my name
I like_ to_ catch my_ feath-ered friends, But that's not where my sto-ry ends;

I___ whis-tle and I___ spread my net, And then some pret - ty_ birds I get,
I___ wish that when I___ spread my net, A hun-dred pret - ty_ girls I'd get,

I___ roam the woods so_ ve - ry free, A_ hap - py man I'll_ al - ways be.
I'd_ choose the fair - est_ one for me, A_ hap - py man I'd_ sure - ly_ be.

Songs for four seasons

Springtime Is a Green Time

Springtime is a green time
   When seedlings start their growing.
Summertime's a rainbow time
   When many blooms are blowing.
Autumntime's a brown time
   When seeds are ripe for sowing:
But wintertime's a white time
(It is the flowers nighttime)
   When stars of frost are glowing.

Rowena Bennett

Swinging Along

Autoharp Chords: F

Traditional

Descant

Swing-ing a-long the o - pen road

C7
Melody

Swing-ing a - long the o - pen road un-der a

F

Swing - ing a - long un - der a sky that's clear.

sky that's clear. Swing-ing a -

Gm

C7

Swing-ing a-long the o - pen road All in the fall, in the

long the o - pen road In the fall of the

F

fall of the year. Swing-ing a - long, swing-ing a - long, swing-ing a -

year. Swing-ing a - long, swing-ing a - long, swing-ing a -

242

long the o-pen road,____ All in the fall of the year.

long the o-pen road All in the fall of the year.

Remember September

Remember September:
  Before she said good-by
She told the youngest robins
  The way they ought to fly.
Around the mountain's shoulder
  She spread a gypsy shawl
And sent a breeze among the trees
  To sing about the fall.

Remember September:
  Before she went away
She taught the cricket fiddlers
  The proper tunes to play.
She gave a modest maple
  A dress of red and gold,
And showed a mouse a little house
  To keep him through the cold.

May Justus

Kröller-Müller Stichting Museum, Otterlo.

Halloween is a time to make and wear things that are both frightening and funny. Artists sometimes produce works that combine both these elements. Of course, what might frighten one person can look funny to another.

Masks that are worn to religious functions are important to the people who wear them, even though they may appear strange to you. Can you think of ways masks have served important purposes in cultures of the past?

Witches are symbols of evil. William Shakespeare
used witches in his play *Macbeth* to predict trouble
and evil events that take place. One scene is introduced
by a roll of thunder. The witches enter and gather around
a flickering fire. On the fire sits a bubbling pot. On page 246
are some lines from the scene that you can accompany
with percussion instruments.

Hallowe'en

Music by Michael Stevens
Words by Harry Behn

1. To - night   is the night   When dead____ leaves fly
2. To - night   is the night   When pump - kins stare

Like   witch - es on   switch - es A - cross   the sky,
Through sheaves____ and   leaves_____ Ev - 'ry - where,

When elf   and   sprite   Flit through____ the   night
When ghoul and   ghost   And gob - lin   host

On   a   moon - y   sheen. } (*A loud*
Dance a - round their queen. } *whisper*)   It's   Hal - lo - we'en!

WITCH 1

    Thrice the brinded cat hath mewed.   *(guiro   )*

WITCH 2

    Thrice, and once the hedge-pig whined.

WITCH 3

    Harpier cries; 'tis time, 'tis time.   *(voice)*

WITCH 1

    Round about the cauldron go;
    In the poisoned entrails throw.   *(drum: thud sounds)*
    Toad, that under cold stone
    Days and nights has thirty-one
    Sweltered venom sleeping got,
    Boil thou first i' th' charmèd pot.   *(maracas: softly shaken)*

ALL

    Double, double, toil and trouble;   *(sand blocks: stirring sound)*
    Fire burn, and cauldron bubble.

WITCH 2

    Fillet of a fenny snake,
    In the cauldron boil and bake;
    Eye of newt, and toe of frog,
    Wool of bat, and tongue of dog,
    Adder's fork, and blindworm's sting,   *(triangle)*
    Lizard's leg, and howlet's wing—   *(castanet)*
    For a charm of pow'rful trouble,
    Like a hell-broth boil and bubble.   *(cymbal roll)*

ALL

    Double, double, toil and trouble;
    Fire burn, and cauldron bubble.   *(sand blocks)*

WITCH 2

    Cool it with a baboon's blood,
    Then the charm is firm and good.   *(low-pitched bell to toll 12 times for midnight)*

"Road with Cypress and Stars" was painted by Vincent Van Gogh. Van Gogh expressed his feelings about life in his work. Artists who are interested in expressing feelings in a very direct way are called expressionists. How did Van Gogh use the medium of oil paint to express his feelings so strongly?

Since ancient times, man has felt a need to be thankful
for a plentiful harvest. Long ago, people had to spend
much time gathering food. In the fall, when the harvest
was in, it seemed appropriate to be thankful for a
good crop.

Thanksgiving Song

Music *by* Jessie Gaynor
Words *by* Alice Riley

1. Swing the shin - ing sick - le, Cut the rip - ened grain,
2. Pick the ros - y ap - ples, Pack a - way with care,
3. Loud - ly blows the north wind Through the shiv-'ring trees,

Flash it in the sun - light, Swing it once a - gain,
Gath - er in the corn ears, Gleam - ing ev - 'ry - where.
Bare are all the branch - es, Fall - en all the leaves.

Tie the gol - den grain - heads In - to shin - ing sheaves,
Now the fruits are gath - ered, All the grains are in,
Gath - ered is the har - vest For an - oth - er year,

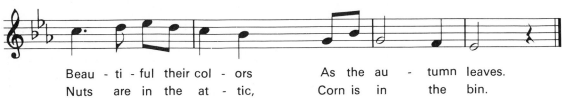

Beau - ti - ful their col - ors As the au - tumn leaves.
Nuts are in the at - tic, Corn is in the bin.
Now our day of glad - ness, Thanks - giv - ing Day, is here.

Praise, O Praise

Traditional English Hymn
Arranged by George Webster

Descant

1. Praise, praise our God and King! Hymns of___ ad - or - a - tion sing!
2. Praise Him that made the sun, Day by___ day its course to run;

Melody

1. Praise, O Praise our God___ and___ King! Hymns of ad - o - ra - tion sing!
2. Praise Him that hath made the___ sun, Day by day its course to run;

For His mer - cies___ shall en - dure, Ev - er___ faith-ful, ev - er sure!

For His___ mer - cies shall en - dure, Ev - er___ faith-ful, ev - er sure!

Chanukah Is Here

Words and music by Alan Mills

1. Cha - nu - kah,   Cha - nu - kah,   Cha - nu - kah   is   here!
2. Cha - nu - kah,   Cha - nu - kah,   Cha - nu - kah   has   come!

Cha - nu - kah,   Cha - nu - kah,   Wel - come with   good   cheer!
Cha - nu - kah,   Cha - nu - kah,   is   the   time   for   fun!

Young and   old   the   gifts   are   bring - ing,   Hear their   joy - ful
Can - dles   glow   on   the   Men - or - ah,   As   we   sing and

voic - es   sing - ing,   For   the   Feast   of   Cha - nu - kah's   the
dance the   ho - ra,   For   the   Feast   of   Cha - nu - kah   brings

gay - est   time   of   year!   For   the   Feast   of
joy   to   ev - 'ry - one!   For   the   Feast   of

Cha - nu - kah's   the   gay - est   time   of   year!
Cha - nu - kah   brings joy   to   ev - 'ry - one!

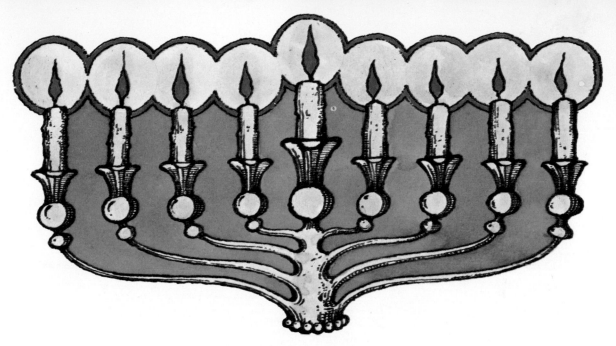

The Hebrew festival of lights is known as Chanukah. It is an eight-day celebration which takes place in December. For the Jewish people, this festival is one of the most joyous holidays.

In the year 168 B.C., the Syrian king Antiochus invaded Jerusalem. He tried to force the Jews to give up their belief in one God and to worship pagan idols. The Jews, under the leadership of Judas Maccabeus, revolted against Antiochus. The Hebrew rebels defeated the Syrians and recovered the temple and the Holy City of Jerusalem.

After the victory, the Hebrews prepared to rededicate the temple. According to legend, when the time came to light the temple lamp, it was discovered that there was enough sacred oil to last only one day. Miraculously, the oil lasted eight days until fresh oil could be prepared.

Each year during the festival of Chanukah, this event is celebrated. Every evening for eight days, an additional candle is lit on the menorah. The menorah is a candlestick with eight stems plus a center stem holding the shammash which is used to light each candle.

A Christmas Greeting

Round by C. A. R.
Words by Sir Walter Scott

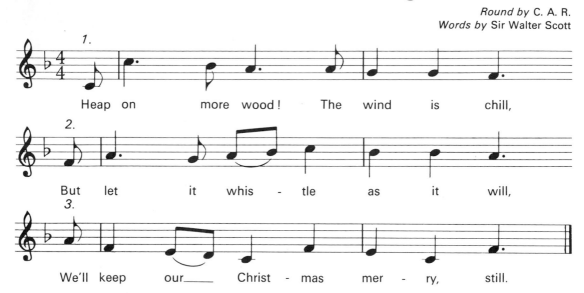

1. Heap on more wood! The wind is chill,

2. But let it whis - tle as it will,

3. We'll keep our___ Christ - mas mer - ry, still.

Christmas Is Remembering

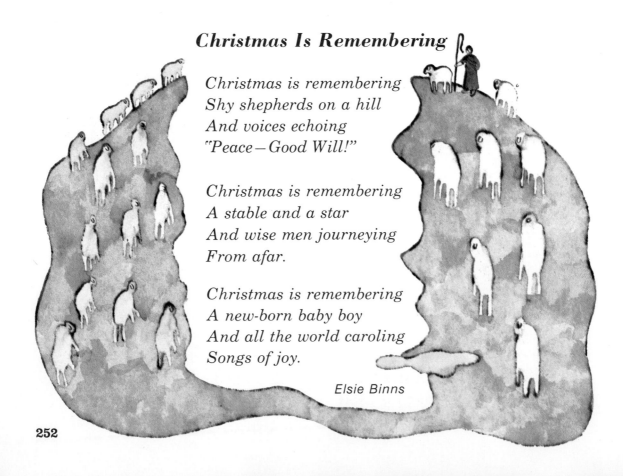

Christmas is remembering
Shy shepherds on a hill
And voices echoing
"Peace—Good Will!"

Christmas is remembering
A stable and a star
And wise men journeying
From afar.

Christmas is remembering
A new-born baby boy
And all the world caroling
Songs of joy.

Elsie Binns

Christmas customs vary from country to country and from age to age. In England, during the Middle Ages, the landowners would entertain all their friends, tenants, and members of their household during the holidays. The great houses were decorated with holly and ivy, and huge yule logs burned as the guests gathered to share the banquet.

The Holly and the Ivy

Old English Carol

1. The hol - ly and the i - vy, when they are both full grown,
2. The hol - ly bears a prick - le as sharp as an - y thorn,
3. The hol - ly bears a ber - ry as red as an - y blood,

Of___ all the trees that are in the wood, the___ hol - ly bears the crown.
And_ Ma - ry bore sweet_ Je - sus Christ on___ Christ - mas Day in the morn.
And_ Ma - ry bore sweet_ Je - sus to___ do poor sin - ners good.

Refrain

Oh, the ris - ing of the sun___ and the run - ning of the deer,

The___ play - ing of the mer - ry or - gan, sweet sing - ing of the choir.

In some countries, the Christmas celebrations last for twelve days, from Christmas Eve through January 6, the feast of Epiphany. Epiphany is the celebration of the Three Kings who came bringing gifts to the Christ child. "The Twelve Days of Christmas" describes the custom of exchanging gifts on each day of the celebration.

The Twelve Days of Christmas

Traditional English Carol

1. On the first day of Christ-mas my true love sent to me: A par - tridge in a pear tree. 2. On the sec-ond day of Christ- mas my true love sent to me: Two tur-tle doves and a par - tridge in a pear tree.

3. On the third day of Christ-mas my true love sent to me: Three French hens, Two tur-tle doves and a par - tridge in a pear tree.

4. On the fourth day of Christ - mas my true love sent to me:

{ Four col-ly birds,
Three French hens, } Two tur-tle doves and a par - tridge in a pear tree.

5. On the fifth day of Christ - mas my true love sent to me:

Five gold-en rings, four— col - ly birds, three French hens,

two— tur - tle doves, and a par - tridge in a pear tree.

Fine

6-12. On the sixth day of Christ - mas my true love sent to me:
(*etc.*)

D.S. al Fine

6. Six   geese   a - lay - ing,
7. Seven   swans   a - swim - ming,
8. Eight   maids   a - milk - ing,
9. Nine   drum - mers drum - ming,
10. Ten   pip - ers   pip - ing,
11. Eleven   la - dies   danc - ing,
12. Twelve   lords   a - leap - ing,

Posada is the Spanish word for inn or shelter.
Las Posadas are the songs of those seeking shelter.

According to ancient legend, the journey of Mary and
Joseph to Bethlehem took nine days. This journey is
dramatized in the Mexican celebration *Las Posadas.* Nine
nights before Christmas, a procession of singers winds in
and out of homes, first stopping at each door to ask for
shelter. After many disappointments, the pilgrims are
invited in for refreshments. The song "Quién les da
Posada" is sung by the people in the procession.

Quién les da Posada

Mexican Folk Song

Canta Exterior: ¿Quién les da posada a estos peregrinos que vienen cansados de andar los caminos?

Canta Interior: Por más que digáis que venís rendidos no damos posadas a desconocidos.

The first part of the song is marked *Canta Exterior*, meaning that it is to be sung outside the house. The second part, *Canta Interior*, is sung within the house. Here is an English translation of the words.

Who Will Give Shelter

Sung Outside:
Who will give shelter
To these pilgrims
Who come tired
From walking the roads?

Sung Inside:
For all that you say
That you come exhausted
We don't give shelter
To unknown ones.

The Christmas Story is the subject of Jan Brueghel's painting "Adoration of the Kings." Although Brueghel showed us many details, the work is unified. Notice how your eyes move from the group around the Infant, to the background figures, and then return to the main group. What device does Brueghel use to lead your eyes around his painting in this way?

Joy to the World

Music arranged from George F. Handel *by* Lowell Mason
Words by Isaac Watts (from Psalm 98)

Descant

1. Joy to the world! the Lord— is— come; Let earth— re -
2. Joy to the world! the sav - ior— reigns; Let men— their—
3. He rules the world with truth— and— grace, And makes the—

Melody

1. Joy to the world! the Lord is come; Let earth re -
2. Joy to the world! the Sav - ior reigns; Let men their
3. He rules the world with truth and grace, And makes the

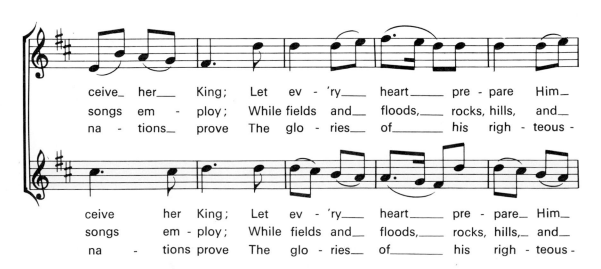

ceive— her— King; Let ev - 'ry— heart— pre - pare Him—
songs em - ploy; While fields and— floods,— rocks, hills, and—
na - tions— prove The glo - ries— of— his righ - teous -

ceive her King; Let ev - 'ry— heart— pre - pare— Him—
songs em - ploy; While fields and— floods,— rocks, hills,— and—
na - tions prove The glo - ries— of— his righ - teous -

room,___   Heav'n and na - ture sing!
plains___   Sing   the sound-ing   joy!
ness,___   Won - ders of   His   love!

room,___ And heav'n and na - ture sing,   And heav'n and na - ture
plains___ Re - peat   the sound-ing_ joy,   Re - peat   the sound-ing_
ness,___And won - ders of   His_ love,   And won - ders of   His_

Heav'n and na - ture sing!   And heav'n___ and na - ture   sing.
Sing   the sound-ing   joy,   Re - peat____ the sound - ing   joy.
Won - ders of   His   love!   And won - ders of___ His   love.

sing,   And heav'n,   and heav'n___ and na - ture   sing.
joy,   Re - peat,_   re - peat____ the sound - ing   joy.
love,   And won - ders, won - ders of   His   love.

This song is one of the best-known carols. The music
was written by a German composer, Felix Mendelssohn.
The words were written by an Englishman,
Charles Wesley.

Hark! The Herald Angels Sing

Music by Felix Mendelssohn
Words by Charles Wesley

1. Hark! the her - ald an - gels sing,— Glo - ry to the new - born King:
2. Hail, the heav'n-born Prince of Peace! Hail, the Son of right-eous-ness!

Peace on earth, and mer - cy mild,— God and sin - ners rec - on - ciled!
Light and life to all He brings, Ris'n with heal - ing in His wings.

Joy - ful all ye na - tions, rise,— Join the tri - umph of the skies;—
Mild He lays His glo - ry by,— Born that man no more may die,—

With th'an - gel - ic host pro - claim, "Christ is — born in Beth - le - hem."
Born to raise the Sons of earth, Born to — give them sec - ond birth.

Hark! the her - ald an - gels sing, Glo - ry — to the new - born King.

"Adoration of the Shepherds" was painted by Rembrandt. This painting is different from Brueghel's. The Brueghel painting on page 257 presents a vast view of the scene; you almost feel that you are watching a performance of a play. Rembrandt's interpretation is more personal. You almost feel that you are part of the group admiring the Child. What device did Rembrandt use to create this feeling? How did he show that the event was very special?

In many parts of our country, singing traditional carols from other lands is an important part of the Christmas festivities. "Infant Jesus, King of Glory" has become a favorite because of its simple, expressive melody.

Infant Jesus, King of Glory

Polish Carol
Words Adapted

1. In-fant Je - sus, King of Glo - ry, In a low - ly cat-tle stall.
2. In-fant Je - sus, King of Glo - ry, We pro-claim thy ho - ly birth.

Moth -er Ma - ry, there be-side you, Stand-ing watch o'er King of all.
Let us sing now of the sto - ry, Of glad tid - ings, peace on earth.

Shep- herds heard the an-gels sing-ing, Sing - ing car - ols filled with joy,___
Come and join in joy-ful sing-ing, Come and see the Ho - ly Babe,___

Christ the Lord is come to - day. Christ the Lord is come to - day.

Welcome to the New Year

Hey, my lad, ho, my lad!
Here's a New Broom.
Heaven's your housetop
And Earth is your room.

Tuck up your shirtsleeves,
There's plenty to do—
Look at the muddle
That's waiting for you!

Dust in the corners
And dirt on the floor,
Cobwebs still clinging
To window and door.

Hey, my lad, ho, my lad!
Nimble and keen—
Here's your New Broom, my lad!
See you sweep clean.

Eleanor Farjeon

263

In some parts of the world the new year is accompanied by heavy snow falls. This Norwegian folk song is about winter fun.

On the Hillside

Norwegian Folk Song
Text Adapted

1. The snow falls white on this fros - ty night On the
   It falls so light, cov - ers all in sight On the

hill - side, On the hill - side. Then out, young men, come and
hill - side, On the hill - side.

join the fun; Then out, young girls! Come out

ev - 'ry - one. To the hill - side! To the hill - side!

2. Why do you sit by the burning wood?
   To the hillside! To the hillside!
   Come, see the snow glitters, clean and good.
   To the hillside! To the hillside!
   Refrain

3. Come bring your skis, come and join the race
   O'er the hillside! O'er the hillside!
   And feel the cold as it stings the face,
   O'er the hillside. O'er the hillside!
   Refrain

In the year 1602, William Shakespeare's play, *Hamlet*, was first performed. "Tomorrow Is St. Valentine's Day" was a popular song about 400 years ago. It was sung in several plays and operas of that time, including Shakespeare's *Hamlet*.

Tomorrow Is St. Valentine's Day

English Folk Song

The excitement of spring can be seen in this colorful painting by a fifth-grade student. She used her imagination and painted a graceful yellow swan. She made a colored background that looks like stained glass. You can make this type of spring painting by doing the following things.

1. Choose a central figure: this could be a person, animal, tree, or flower. Make the figure large.

2. Move your pencil all over the background to make different shapes of various sizes.

3. Paint your figure in one color; use many colors for the background.

"The May Day Carol" captures the new-found joy
of spring.

The May Day Carol

Traditional English Song

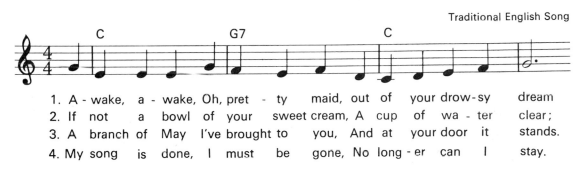

1. A - wake, a - wake, Oh, pret - ty   maid, out of   your drow-sy   dream
2. If   not   a   bowl   of your   sweet cream, A   cup   of   wa - ter   clear ;
3. A   branch of   May   I've brought to   you, And   at   your door it   stands.
4. My   song   is   done,   I   must   be   gone, No long - er   can   I   stay.

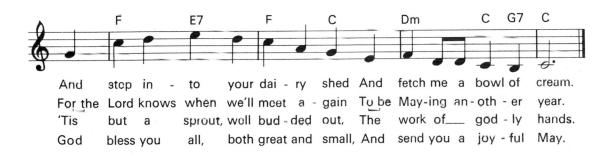

And   step in - to   your dai - ry   shed And   fetch me   a bowl of   cream.
For the Lord knows when   we'll meet a - gain   To be May-ing an - oth - er   year.
'Tis   but   a   sprout, well bud - ded out,   The   work of___ god - ly   hands.
God   bless you   all,   both great and   small, And   send you a   joy - ful   May.

Accompany the song with this recorder or bell descant.

In 1790 John Trumbull painted this portrait of George Washington. It shows the General in his army uniform. What did Trumbull do in this painting to show that General Washington was a great leader, yet not too different from other people?

268

Music of my country

The lines of the poem below express a deep loyalty to the poet's homeland.

My Native Land

Breathes there the man, with soul so dead
Who never to himself hath said,
   This is my own, my native land!
Whose heart hath ne'er within him burned,
As home his footsteps he hath turned,
   From wandering on a foreign strand!

Sir Walter Scott

It is a special moment when our national anthem, "The Star-Spangled Banner," is sung.

A national anthem should never be applauded. Standing and singing the song proudly is the best way to show respect for your country.

The Star-Spangled Banner

Music Attributed to J. S. Smith
Words by Francis Scott Key

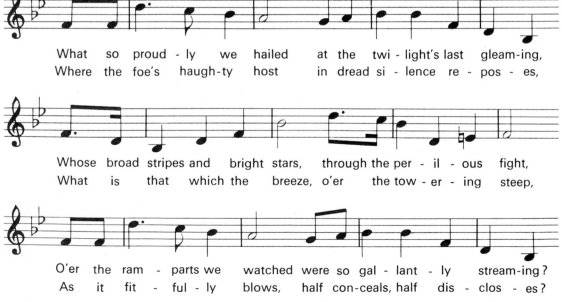

1. Oh,___ say! can you see, by the dawn's ear - ly light,
2. On the shore, dim - ly seen through the mists of the deep,

What so proud - ly we hailed at the twi - light's last gleam-ing,
Where the foe's haugh-ty host in dread si - lence re - pos - es,

Whose broad stripes and bright stars, through the per - il - ous fight,
What is that which the breeze, o'er the tow - er - ing steep,

O'er the ram - parts we watched were so gal - lant - ly stream-ing?
As it fit - ful - ly blows, half con-ceals, half dis - clos - es?

And the rock - ets' red glare, the bombs burst - ing in air,
Now it catch - es the gleam of the morn - ing's first beam,

Gave proof through the night that our flag was still there.
In full glo - ry re - flec-ted now__ shines on the stream;

Oh, say, does that__ Star - Span - gled Ban - ner__ yet__ wave__
'Tis the Star - Span - gled__ Ban - ner, oh, long may__ it___ wave__

O'er the land_____ of the free and the home of the brave?
O'er the land_____ of the free and the home of the brave!

America was founded by those seeking freedom.
Today, many still look toward this nation with the hope
of being free.

The universal search for peace and freedom is expressed
in the song "Let There Be Peace on Earth."

Let There Be Peace on Earth

Words and music by Sy Miller and Jill Jackson

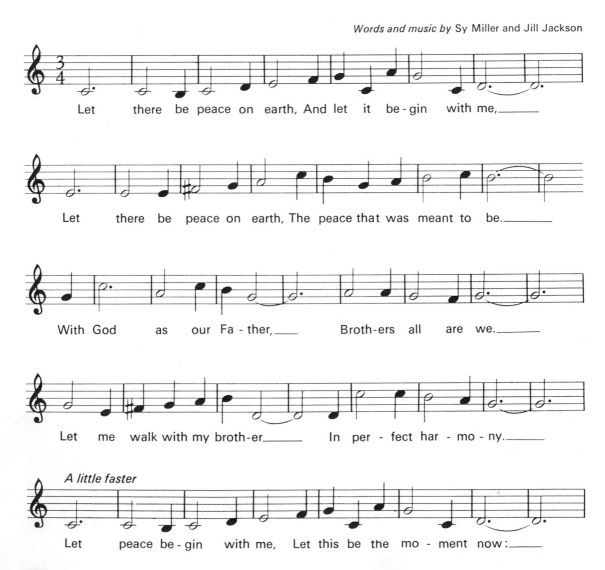

a little slower

With ev-'ry step I take, Let this be my sol-emn vow:____

Broadly

To take each mo - ment and live each mo - ment

In peace e - ter - nal - ly._____ Let there be peace on earth

And let it be - gin with me._____

The theme of peace is one that also concerns artists. There are many ways of expressing a desire for peace. One way is to show the horror of war. An-other is to show how joyous life would be if the world were peaceful. How did Pablo Picasso express his desire for peace in this painting?

Shortly before the time of the American Civil War, the Reverend William Whiting wrote the words for the song which was to become known as the Navy Hymn. This song was officially adopted by the United States Naval Academy at Annapolis. The song has also become a part of the British and French naval traditions.

Eternal Father, Strong to Save

Music by John B. Dykes
Words by William Whiting

1. E - ter - nal Fa - ther, strong to save, Whose arm doth bind the
2. O Trin - i - ty of love and power, Our breth - ren shield in

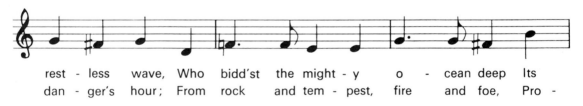

rest - less wave, Who bidd'st the might - y o - cean deep Its
dan - ger's hour; From rock and tem - pest, fire and foe, Pro -

own ap - point - ed lim - its keep: O hear us when we
tect them where - so - e'er they go: Thus ev - er - more shall

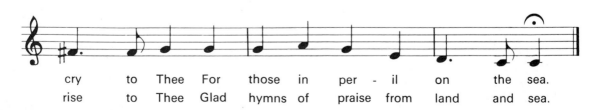

cry to Thee For those in per - il on the sea.
rise to Thee Glad hymns of praise from land and sea.

Navy Hymn
Arranged for Orchestra and Choir

What happens in the recording to make the second
verse different from the first verse?

American Heritage

The Declaration of Independence,
The Constitution with its Bill of Rights:
These are the bulwarks of our heritage,
These are our nation's guiding lights.

Freedom of speech, freedom of press,
Freedom to worship as we please,
The right to assemble, the right to petition,
Are some of the freedoms we recite with ease.

The right to life, the right to liberty,
The right to the pursuit of happiness,
The right to equality, the right to security,
The right to live without undue stress.

But what of the many other rights,
Not written in our laws:
The right to labor, the right to suffer,
The right to fight for freedom's cause?

For these are rights our forefathers chose,
When they laid our country's foundation,
And these are the rights we must assume
To preserve our precious nation.

Elsie Walush

More Choral Music

You're a Grand Old Flag   *278*
Watah Come a Me Eye   *280*
How Good It Is to Sing Together   *283*
It's Such a Joy   *284*
A Tired Cowboy   *285*
Texas, Our Texas   *287*
Aardvarks on the Ark   *289*

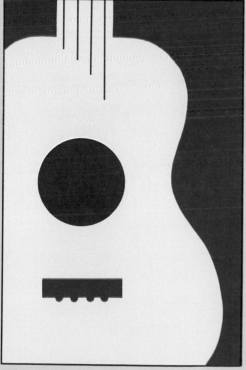

Playing the Ukulele

Are You Sleeping?   *298*
Down in the Valley   *299*
The Streets of Laredo   *300*
Cuckoo   *301*
Hawaiian Surf   *302*
Farewell to Thee   *304*
Holla Hi, Holla Ho   *306*
Mahalo Nui   *307*
Never Argue with a Bee   *309*
My Home's in Montana   *310*
Old Joe Clark   *311*
Camptown Races   *312*
Mary Ann   *313*

You're a Grand Old Flag

George M. Cohan
Arr. by Mary Val Marsh

2nd time only: Part I

There is a flag, a ver-y high fly-ing flag,

1st time: All voices unison
2nd time: Part II

You're a grand old flag, You're a high fly-ing flag, And for-

Ev - er will it wave,

ev - er in peace may you wave, You're the

It's the no-ble em-blem of the na-tion that I love,

em - blem of the land I love, the

(A few voices) Let her wave!

Free and brave,

home of the free and the brave, Ev - 'ry

All hearts beat true be-fore the Red, White, and Blue,

heart beats true, un-der Red, White, and Blue, Where there's

Nev – er boast or brag, But should auld ac-quaint-ance

nev – er a boast or brag, But should auld ac-quaint-ance

1.

be for-got, just keep your eye on that

be for-got, keep your eye on that grand old flag.

2. *rit.*

(div.)

flag, Keep your eye on that grand old flag!

flag, Keep your eye on that grand old flag!

*Optional third part.

Watah Come a Me Eye

West Indian Folk Song
Collected by Lois Hassell-Habteyes
Arr. by Mary Val Marsh

1. Ev-'ry time I 'mem-bah Li-za, Wa-tah come_ a me eye;
(Wa-ter comes to my eye)

When I think 'bout my guhl Li-za, Wa-tah come_ a me eye.
(girl)

(Double pattern if possible:)

Refrain

Come back, Li-za, come back_ guhl,_ Wa-tah come_ a me eye;

280

Cl.

Mar.

C   G7   C

Come back, Li-za, come back_ guhl,_ Wa-tah come_ a me eye.

25

Claves

Bongos

Guiro (opt.)

Voices   (Continue claves, bongos and guiro to end)

Countermelody

29 C   G7   C   G7

Come back, my Li-za, back home! Come back, my Li-za, back home!

33 C   G7

Come back, my Li-za, back home! Oh, how_ I miss

2. Since you gone duh days been lone-ly, Wa-tah come_ a me
          (the)

C

my lit-tle Li-za. Come back, my Li-za, back home!

eye;   Come back guhl I love you on-ly,

How Good It Is to Sing Together

Traditional Israeli Round
Acc. by M. Rinehart
English text by Alan Mills (CAPAC)

With enthusiasm ♩. = 84

① Dm / Gm / Dm / Gm / A7

How good it is, my {bro - thers,} {sis - ters,} to meet— and sing to -

Dm

geth - er. How good it is, my {bro - thers,} {sis - ters,} to

②

meet— and sing to - geth - er. Oh, how

good it is to meet— and sing to - geth - er. Oh, how

good it is to meet— and sing to - geth - er.

Add this countermelody.

Come, my {bro - thers,} {sis - ters,} meet and sing to - geth - er.

It's Such a Joy

Words and Music by Carrol Rinehart
Acc. by Herbert Allen

It's such a joy to come and sing a - long with you.___ There's not an-oth - er thing that I would rath-er do.___ So lift your voice in song, come and sing a - long,___ A song for me and for you. It's such a- you.___ A song for me and for you.___

1.2.3.

4.

Coda
unison

divisi

A Tired Cowboy

Words and Music by Paula Karchmer
Arr. by Carroll Rinehart
Acc. by Herbert Allen

head.   I don't want to ride a - gain 'Til the

head.   I don't want to ride a - gain 'Til the

sun's up in the sky. Got-ta rest my wear-y bones or I'll die.

sun's up in the sky. Got-ta rest my wear-y bones or I'll die.

___ Roll-in' home _____ rid-in' from the range.___

___ Roll-in' home___   roll - in'

___ Get-tin' kind-a tired_____ an' I wan-na go to

home   Get-tin' kind-a tired,   wan-na go to

                    p

bed.___   And I wan-na go to bed.___

                    p

bed.___   And I wan-na go to bed.___

Texas, Our Texas

Words by Gladys Yoakum Wright
Music by William J. Marsh
Descant by MVM

Allegro maestoso (with steady march rhythm - not fast)
(Optional descant – Use verse 3 only if more than one verse is used)

1. Tex - as, our Tex-as, All hail, might-y State!
3. Tex - as, dear Tex-as, From ty - rant now free.

Melody

1. Tex - as, our Tex-as! All hail the might-y State!
2. Tex - as, O Tex-as! Your free-born Sin-gle Star,
3. Tex - as, dear Tex-as! From ty - rant grip now free,

Tex - as, our Tex - as, So won - drous great.
Shines forth in splen-dor Your Des - ti - ny!

cresc.

Tex - as, our Tex - as! So won-der-ful so great!
Sends out its ra-diance To na-tions near and far,
Shines forth in splen-dor Your Star of Des - ti - ny!

Bold and grand - est, A - gainst each test; O
Mo - ther of he - roes, Your child - ren true Pro-

Bold-est and grand-est, With-stand-ing ev - 'ry test; O
Em - blem of Free-dom! It sets our hearts a - glow, With
Mo - ther of He - roes! We come your chil-dren true, Pro-

cresc.   *f*   *rall.*

Em - pire wide and glo-rious, Su-preme - ly blest.
claim - ing our al - le-giance, Our Love for you.

cresc.   *f*   *rall.*

Em - pire wide and glo-rious, You stand su-preme-ly blest.
thoughts of San Ja - cin - to And glo - rious Al - a - mo.
claim - ing our al - le-giance Our Faith Our Love for you.

Refrain

21 *p a tempo*

God bless Tex - as! And keep you strong, That

p a tempo

God bless you Tex - as! And keep you brave and strong, That

you may grow Through-out ag - es long.

you may grow in pow'r and worth, Through-out the ag - es long.

29 *ff*

God bless Tex - as And keep you strong, That

ff

God bless you Tex - as! And keep you brave and strong, That

you may grow_____ Through-out the ag - es long.

you may grow in pow'r and worth Through-out the ag - es long.

288

Aardvarks on the Ark

(or "How Did Noah Stand It?")

Mary Val Marsh
Based on a spiritual

($\quad$ = 126)

Who built the ark! No - ah, No - ah;

Who built the ark? Broth-er No - ah built the ark. Say!

No - ah built the ark. He had

an - i - mals of ev - 'ry size and shape! He had

an - i-mals of ev - 'ry kind that you can name. He had you can name.

Bongos (same tempo as above)
R.H.
L.H.

Spoken, in rhythm
with expressive inflection

Group I

1. There were
2. There were

crick-ets small, gi-raffes so tall, and an-te-lopes and liz - ards!
big black bears and kan - ga-roos, and el - e-phants and AARD-VARKS!

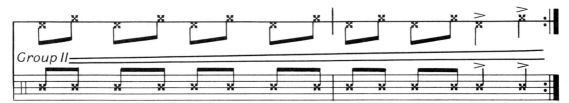

Group II

Ze-bras striped and pea-cocks bright, and an - i - mals with giz - zards!
Small rac - coons and por - cu - pines, and cats and dogs, but NO SHARKS!

Bongos (3 times)

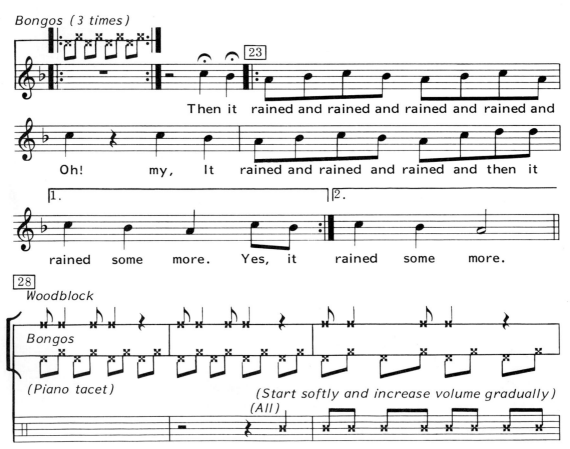

Then it rained and rained and rained and rained and

Oh! my, It rained and rained and rained and then it

|1.

rained some more. Yes, it

|2.

rained some more.

28

Woodblock

Bongos

(Piano tacet)

(Start softly and increase volume gradually)
(All)

Now once a - board that gi-ant boat they

290

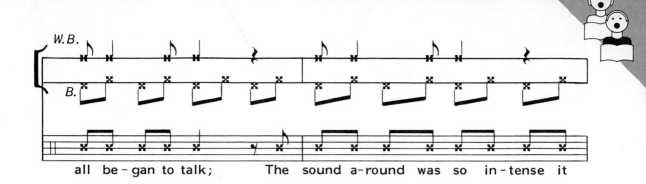

all be-gan to talk; The sound a-round was so in-tense it

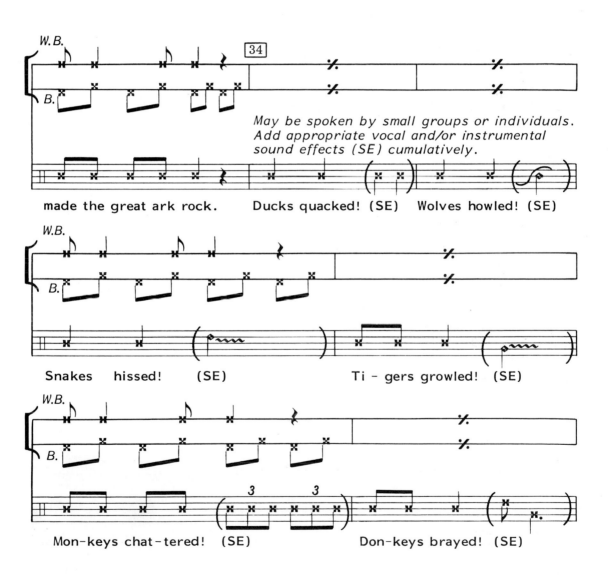

made the great ark rock.　Ducks quacked! (SE)　Wolves howled! (SE)

*May be spoken by small groups or individuals.
Add appropriate vocal and/or instrumental
sound effects (SE) cumulatively.*

Snakes　hissed!　(SE)　　Ti - gers growled!　(SE)

Mon-keys chat-tered!　(SE)　　Don-keys brayed! (SE)

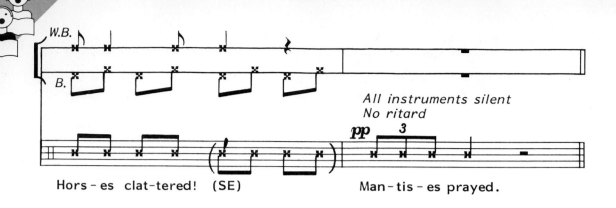

All instruments silent
No ritard

Hors-es clat-tered! (SE)   Man-tis-es prayed.

42

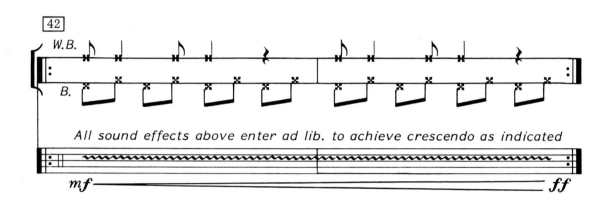

All sound effects above enter ad lib. to achieve crescendo as indicated

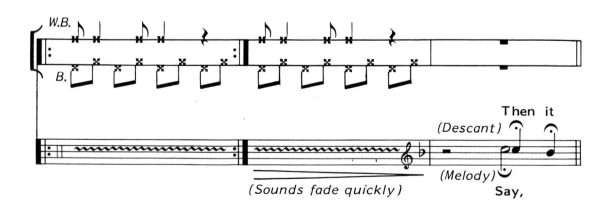

(Sounds fade quickly)

Then it
(Descant)
(Melody)
Say,

47 *Bongos and woodblock resume patterns; play to end.*

rained and rained and rained and rained and Oh! my, It

Who built the ark? No - ah, No - ah,

1. *no ritard.*

rained and rained and rained and then it rained some more. Yes, it

Who built the ark? Broth - er No - ah built the ark. Say,

2. **52**

rained some more. Broth - er No - ah

No-ah built the ark. Broth - er No - ah

W. B.

B.

built the ark.

(opt.)

built the ark.

Playing the Ukulele

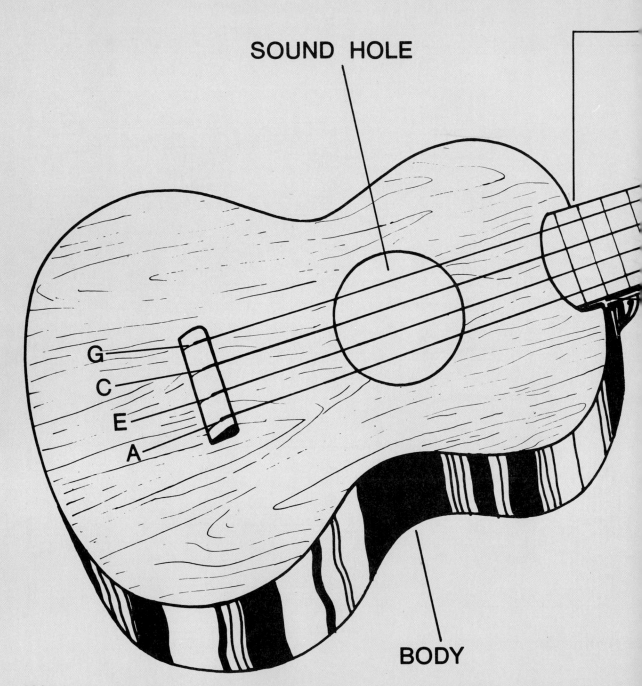

SOUND HOLE

G
C
E
A

BODY

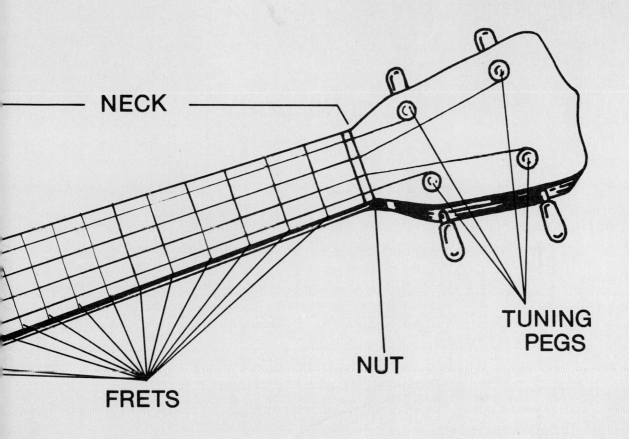

NECK

FRETS

NUT

TUNING PEGS

The ukulele is a musical instrument from Hawaii. The Portuguese sailors who came to the Pacific Islands about a hundred years ago brought with them a type of guitar called the *machete*. The machete is the ancestor of the ukulele.

Because the uke is small, easy to carry, and easy to play, it is a popular instrument for accompanying songs at parties and picnics. The term "uke" is a short form of "ukulele."

The ukulele's strings may be tuned to these pitches.

To tune your uke, play the note on the piano that gives the pitch of each string. Tighten each string by turning the peg until you reach the correct pitch. If you tune a string too high, loosen the peg a bit. When you have tuned all four strings, you are ready to play.

Form a C with the thumb and middle finger of your left hand. Slip the neck of the uke between these fingers, with the back of the uke neck resting on your thumb. Be sure to keep your thumb relaxed. If you keep your fingers curved over the strings, it will be easier to change chords.

Your right hand is used to **strum.** A strum is a downward stroke across all four strings. Use the thumb or first two fingers of the right hand to strum.

Uke players use fingering charts or **tablatures** to show them where to place the fingers of their left hand. The tablature is a diagram of the uke neck which shows the strings and the frets.

The picture below shows the finger numbers that are indicated on the tablature. Since the thumb of the left hand is used only to hold the instrument, the numbering starts with the index finger.

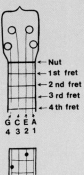

Tablatures

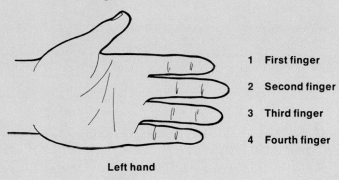

1   **First finger**

2   **Second finger**

3   **Third finger**

4   **Fourth finger**

Left hand

The **frets** are guides for your fingers. To play a chord, place your fingers between the frets. The black dots on the tablature show you where to place your fingers to play a particular chord.

Here is the tablature for the F major chord. To play the F major chord:

1. Place the first finger on the second string between the nut and the first fret.

2. Place your second finger on the fourth string between the first and second frets.

3. Press hard enough for the strings to touch the uke neck, but not so hard that your hand gets tired.

4. The other strings are **open.** This means that no part of your hand should touch these strings.

Practice strumming:

You can use the F major chord to accompany "Are You Sleeping?" Think of the rhythm of the song. Where do the strong pulses occur? Strum all four strings lightly on each strong pulse.

Are You Sleeping?

Traditional

Are you sleep-ing, are you sleep-ing, Broth-er John, Broth-er John?

Morn-ing bells are ring - ing, Morn-ing bells are ring - ing,

Ding, ding, dong, ding, ding, dong.

Both the F chord and the C7 chord are needed to accompany "Down in the Valley." To play C7:

1. Place the first finger on the first string between the nut and the first fret.

2. The other three strings are open. Strum all four of the strings.

Practice moving your fingers from the F chord to the C7 chord.

298

Look at "Down in the Valley." The chord names are written above the staff. If you forget where to place your fingers for these chords, look at the tablatures.

While you prepare to accompany a song, it is a good idea to think of the tempo of the song before you begin to play. If the song is slow, such as "Down in the Valley," you may want to strum on each strong pulse (three times per measure).

Down in the Valley

Southern Folk Song

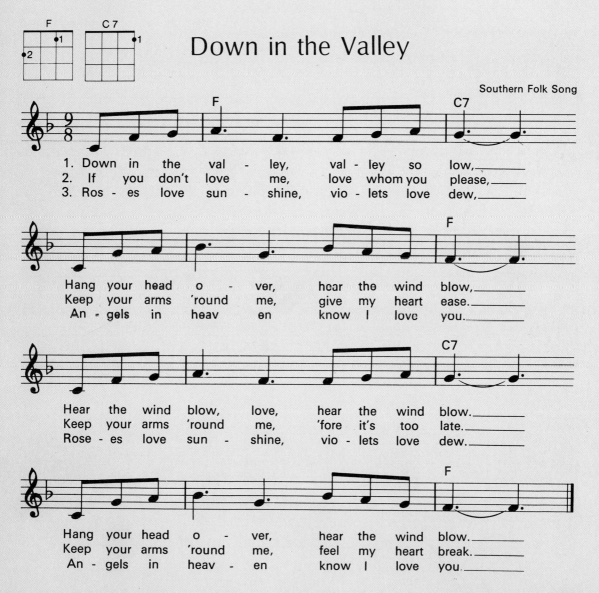

1. Down in the val - ley, val - ley so low,_____
2. If you don't love me, love whom you please,_____
3. Ros - es love sun - shine, vio - lets love dew,_____

Hang your head o - ver, hear the wind blow,_____
Keep your arms 'round me, give my heart ease._____
An - gels in heav - en know I love you._____

Hear the wind blow, love, hear the wind blow._____
Keep your arms 'round me, 'fore it's too late._____
Rose - es love sun - shine, vio - lets love dew._____

Hang your head o - ver, hear the wind blow._____
Keep your arms 'round me, feel my heart break._____
An - gels in heav - en know I love you._____

"The Streets of Laredo" is a sad cowboy song. You can accompany it with F and C7 chords. Strum on each metric beat or on the strong pulse of each measure.

The Streets of Laredo

Cowboy song

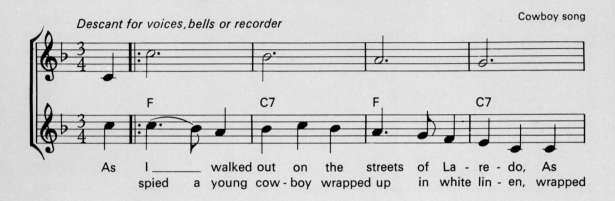

Descant for voices, bells or recorder

As   I _____ walked out   on   the   streets   of La - re - do,   As
spied   a   young cow - boy wrapped up   in white lin - en, wrapped

I _____ walked out   in   La - re - do   one   day,   I
up   in white

lin - en   as   cold   as   the   clay.

"Cuckoo" is an Austrian folk song. The song may be
accompanied on the ukulele with the F and C7 chords.
How often per measure will you strum?

Cuckoo

Austrian Folk Song
Words Adapted

1. Oh, I went down to the wood-land brook, Where the wa - ter's so
2. Af - ter Eas - ter come__ sun - ny days That will melt with the
3. When I've mar - ried my__ maid - en fair What then can I de-

good; And I heard there the cuck - oo As she called from the
snow; Then I'll mar - ry my maid-en fair, We'll be hap - py I
sire; Oh, a home for her tend - ing And some wood for the

wood.⎫ Ho - la - ah ho - le-ra-hi = hi - ah, Ho - le-rah, cuck-oo,
know.⎬
fire.⎭

Ho - le-ra - hi - hi - ah, Ho - le-rah, cuck - oo, ho - le-rah - hi - hi - ah,

Ho - le - rah cuck-oo, Ho - le-rah - hi - hi - ah ho.

301

The B♭ major chord is needed to accompany "Hawaiian Surf." To play B♭ major:

1. Use the first finger to press both the first and second strings between the nut and the first fret.

2. Use the second finger to press the third string between the first and second frets.

3. Use the third finger to press the fourth string between the second and third frets.

Practice changing chords:

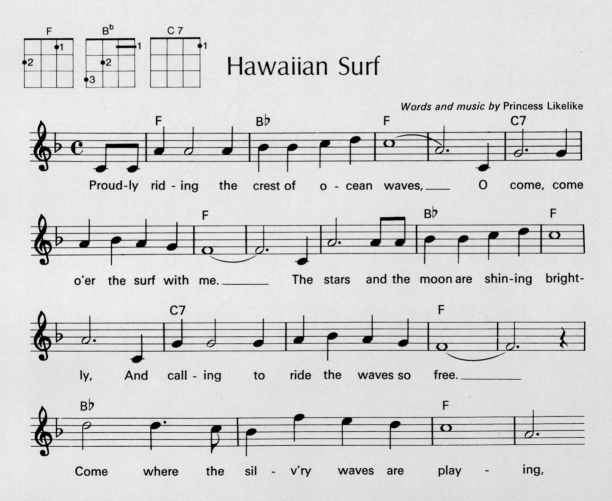

Hawaiian Surf

Words and music by **Princess Likelike**

Proud-ly rid - ing the crest of o - cean waves, ____ O come, come

o'er the surf with me. ____ The stars and the moon are shin-ing bright-

ly, And call - ing to ride the waves so free. ____

Come where the sil - v'ry waves are play - ing,

O'er the surf, o'er the surf___ with___ me.___

Breez - es are mur - m'ring, moon - light beam - ing,

Through the cool spray, The spray___ of the sea.___

You probably have noticed by now that it is very important to listen carefully to the singers you are accompanying. If you find that the group is falling behind or getting ahead of the accompanist, it may be necessary to adjust your tempo. It may be helpful for the uke player to give a few strums to set the tempo of the song and to give the starting pitch to the singers. For example, an introduction to "Hawaiian Surf" might be played something like this.

UKE:

VOICES:

Proud-ly rid - ing the crest of

Pali is an Hawaiian name for a cliff. One very famous *pali* is located in a mountain pass a few miles from Honolulu. Strong winds blow through the pass. From the edge of the *pali* one can look toward the ocean and see beautiful green meadows and towering mountains.

Practice strumming:

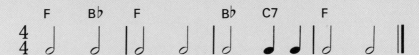

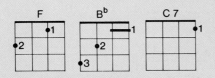

Farewell to Thee
(Aloha Oe)

Words and music by Queen Liliuokalani

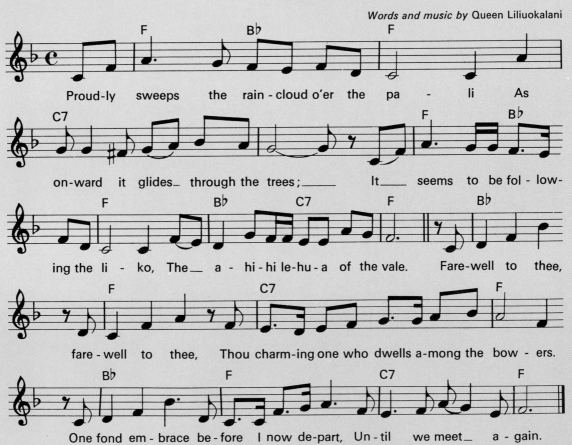

Proud-ly sweeps the rain-cloud o'er the pa - li As on-ward it glides through the trees; It seems to be fol-low-ing the li - ko, The a - hi-hi le-hu-a of the vale. Fare-well to thee, fare-well to thee, Thou charm-ing one who dwells a-mong the bow - ers. One fond em - brace be-fore I now de-part, Un-til we meet a - gain.

To play the C major chord, place your third finger on the first string between the second and third frets.

Practice strumming:

C

To play the G7 chord:

1. Place your third finger on the first string between the first and second frets.

2. Place your first finger on the second string between the nut and the first fret.

3. Place your second finger on the third string between the first and second frets.

Practice strumming:

G 7

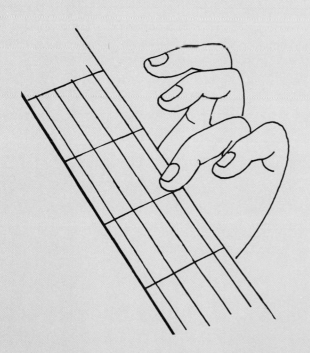

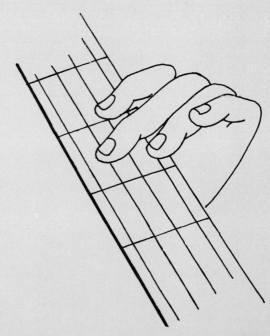

"Holla Hi, Holla Ho" is a good song to sing on a hike.
Where is your favorite place for a hike?

Holla Hi, Holla Ho

German Folk Song
Words Adapted

Who will come with me to - day? Hol - la hi! Hol - la ho!

We'll go hik - ing far a - way, Hol - la, hol - la ho!

We will leave in the ear - ly morn, Hol - la hi! Hol - la ho!

Then come back when the day - light's gone, Hol - la, Hol - la ho!

Mahalo Nui is the Hawaiian way of saying "thank you."
Practice strumming:

Mahalo Nui

Music *by* Carol Roes and Lloyd Stone
Words *by* Carol Roes

Ma - ha - lo Nu - i   For a love - ly hol - i - day,
Ha - wai - ian mem - 'ries   Will_ haunt me ev - er - more,

Ma - ha - lo Nu - i,   As I go a - way.
A fond a - lo - ha,

As I leave your shore.   You gave me flow - er leis,

With Ha-wai - i's smile,   You made the sun - ny days

Seem so worth-while.   Ma - ha - lo Nu - i,

And as I now de-part,   Ma - ha - lo Nu - i,

With all my heart.   With all my heart._____

After you have gained some skill playing the ukulele, you may want to add rhythmic interest to your strumming. One way to do this is to use part of the melodic rhythm of the song. For example, "Streets of Laredo" begins with a dotted rhythm pattern. You could strum the dotted rhythm pattern throughout, providing a rhythmic ostinato for the singing.

or:

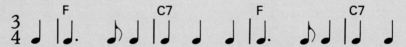

Or, you may prefer to match the melodic rhythm exactly in your strum.

When you strum rapidly, it is easier to brush your thumb or fingers back in the opposite direction rather than to use a down-stroke for each note.

Select a favorite song and experiment with different strumming effects.

The following songs may be played using the chords you have learned. As you play the songs, practice different ways of strumming.

Never Argue with a Bee

Chorus

Words and music by Malvina Reynolds

G7 — Nev - er ar - gue with a bee.
C — He has got a sting-a - ree.

Be he work-er, be he drone, You had best leave him a - lone.

F
1. He has got his work to do, Get-ting hon-ey from the tree.
2. And the wasp is ve - ry wild, If you both-er with his child;

G7
If you know what's good for you, Do not ar - gue with a bee.
Let him go where he is bound, Do not try to mess a - round.

My Home's in Montana

Cowboy Song
Words adapted

1. My home's in Mon - ta - na, I wear a ban - da - na, My
2. When val - leys are dus - ty, My po - ny is trust - y; He
3. When far from the ranch - es, I chop the pine branch - es To

spurs are of sil - ver, My po - ny is gray. When
lopes through the bliz - zard, The snow in his ears. The
heap on my camp - fire As day - light grows pale; when

rid - ing the ran - ges My luck nev - er chan - ges: With
cat - tle may scat - ter, But what does it mat - ter! My
I have par - tak - en of beans and of ba - con, I

foot in the stir - rup I'll gal - lop a - way.
rope is a hal - ter for pig - head - ed steers.
whis - tle a mer - ry old song of the trail.

Old Joe Clark

American Folk Song

1. I went up to old Joe's house, Old Joe was-n't at home,
2. Old Joe had a big red barn, Fif-teen sto-ries high,
3. Old Joe was a fid-dlin' man, Fid-dled his whole-life through,

Ate up all his good roast beef, And threw a-way the bone.
Ev-'ry sto-ry in that barn Was filled with chick-en pie.
On-ly tune he ev-er played Was "Hon-ey, I love you."

Refrain

Round and round, old Joe Clark, Round and round, I say,

Round and round, old Joe Clark, Bet-ter be on my way.

Camptown Races

Words and music by Stephen C. Foster

C
Camp-town la - dies sing this song, Doo - dah, doo - dah.
Went down there with my hat caved in, Doo - dah, doo - dah.

Camp-town race track five miles long, Oh, doo-dah - day.
Came back home with a pock-et-ful of tin, Oh, doo-dah - day.

Goin' to run all night, Goin' to run all day,

Bet my mon-ey on the bob - tailed nag, Some-bod-y bet on the bay.

Mary Ann

Calypso Song

Refrain

All night, all day,__ Miss Ma - ry Ann,_____

Down by__ the sea - side,__ sift - ing sand._____

Ev - ery - bod - y down there__ join the band,_____

Down by__ the sea - side__ sift - ing sand.__ *Fine*

Verse

If you come to our Port of Spain, you'll nev - er want__ to go

home a - gain.__ You'll do ev - er - y - thing you can,__

Just to be__ round Miss Mar - y Ann.__ *D.C. al Fine*

313

The following chart will provide a handy reference for reviewing chord fingerings. It will also be helpful in learning to play additional chords.

Minor Chords

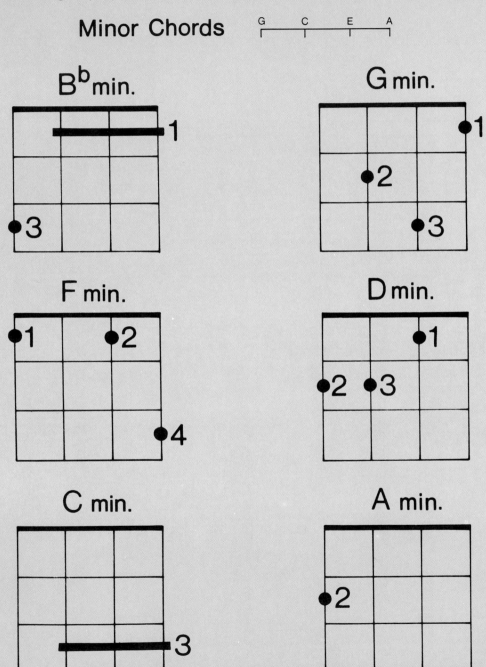

Major Chords

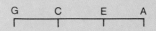
G   C   E   A

B♭
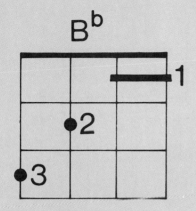

G
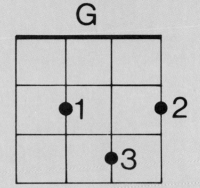

F
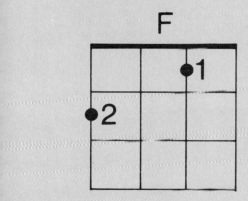

D
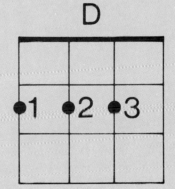

C
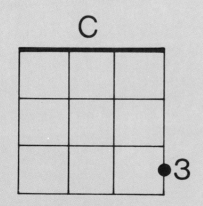

A
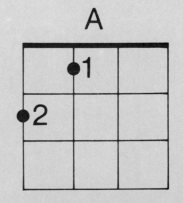

315

Seventh Chords

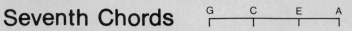

B♭7
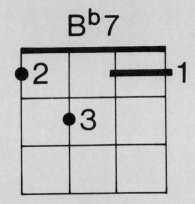

G 7
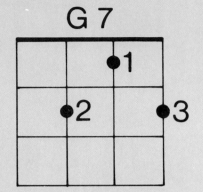

F 7
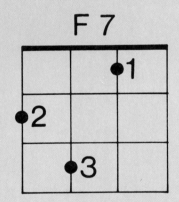

D 7
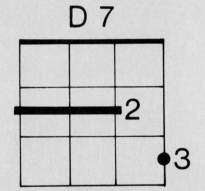

C 7
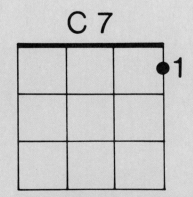

A 7
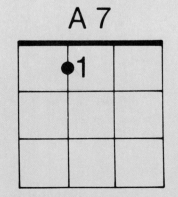

Do You Know?

1. No two voices are alike. This is because each person's voice has a different sound or tone quality which is called its

    a. range   **b.** timbre   **c.** volume

2. Listen to the recording of "He Shall Feed His Flock." Two voices are heard singing this aria. The second one is a soprano. The first one is

    a. a contralto   **b.** a baritone   **c.** a bass

3. Many percussion instruments, such as a maracas and a tambourine, cannot play a melody. But some percussion instruments can play a melody. Examples are:

    a. marimba and celesta   **b.** triangle and gong
               c. xylophone and violin

4. Listen to the recording of the "Farandole" from *L'Arlésienne Suite No. 2*. Listen to the instruments that are playing. Identify at least three of the instruments you hear.

5. Here are some rhythm phrases. One of them does not have the correct number of counts. To help you find which one is wrong, look at the meter signature and count the beats in each measure. Clap each pattern.

Which one is wrong?

6. Listen to the recording of "Never Argue with a Bee" and sing the song.   The first two measures look like this.

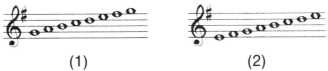

The note with the sharp sign (♯) is called an accidental.   It is called this because

a. this note is not in the key signature.
b. the composer put it into the music by accident.
c. it is a printer's mistake.

7. Here are two scales.   Play them on the piano or the bells.

(1)   (2)

Which scale is a minor scale, number 1 or number 2?

8. You know that a chord is made up of three or more tones played at the same time.   Write a chord that consists of F as the root, and the third and fifth tones above F.

9. If you heard four pieces of music, each written with one of these tempo markings:

presto   largo   allegro   andante

which piece would be the fastest?   the slowest?

10. Listen for the number of phrases in the recording of the song "Pat Works on the Railway."   How many phrases are there in one verse plus the refrain?

a. four   **b.** two   **c.** eight

11. Listen to the recording of the song "Chicka-Hanka."
Behind the melody you hear this rhythm pattern repeated over and over again.

A rhythm or melody pattern that is repeated again and
again in a composition is called

a. a coda   **b.** an ostinato   **c.** harmony

12. A story that is told through music and dance is called

a. a ballerina
b. a ballet
c. a square dance

13. Here is the beginning of a song that you know.

Play this on the bells or piano or sing it. Try to add
your own harmony to this melody. Write the chord
tones on your answer sheet.

14. If you went to a theater and saw and heard singers on
the stage in costume acting out parts, accompanied
by an orchestra, you would know you were attending

a. a concerto
b. an opera
c. an overture

15. What is your favorite musical instrument? Explain
why you like it. What kind of music have you heard
played on this instrument?

Game Time

FOLLOW THE LEADER

Divide into two teams. Members of each team will take turns being the leader and the responder or "echo."

The leader claps a rhythm pattern and chooses some-one from the opposite team to respond. As the leader finishes clapping, he calls "repetition" or "variation." The "echo" must clap the exact pattern if he hears the word "repetition." If "variation" is called, the "echo" must vary the pattern. Scores should be kept for each team, a point given for each correct response.

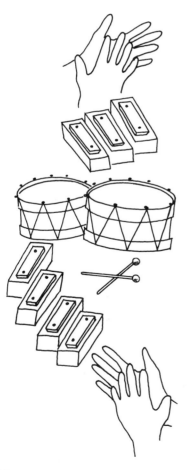

Variations of the game:

a. Use pairs of percussion instruments, one set for the leader, and one set for the "echo." The leader's hands and instruments should be shielded, so the opposing team cannot see them. The leader chooses an instrument and plays a rhythm pattern. The "echo" must (1) remember the rhythm pattern, (2) choose the correct instrument, (3) respond correctly, with repetition or variation.

b. Use two sets of bells, five bells in each set. Again, the leader and bells should be shielded. The leader plays a melody pattern on the bells. The person who responds must (1) remember the pattern, (2) choose bells with the same pitches to play the pattern and (3) respond with repetition or variation as before.

FUN WITH LETTERS

1. The music alphabet is ABCDEFG. There are at least 55 words that can be made from these letters. Here are just a few:

ABCDEFG

BADGE	**CEDED**	**FADED**
AGED	**DEAF**	**EDGE**
DEEDED	**BAGGAGE**	**CAGED**

Make a list of five words, using the music alphabet. Play these, one at a time on bells or piano for your friends. Tell them only the first letter of the word you are going to play. Have them figure out the word by listening very carefully to the melody. If they know the music alphabet they will be able to do this.

2. Choose the word that sounds best to you. Write the word in music notation. Use it and two other words as the basis for a melody. Write your melody, then add a flat or a sharp here and there to make it more interesting. Play your melody for others. You can do this by yourselves or as a class.

3. Write words as chords, to be read from the bottom note up. Each person might have one word ready to use. You can also try playing the chords instead of writing them. This will be more difficult.

Say It with Movement

ADD A MOVEMENT

You can play an "add a movement" game, and turn it into a dance. Divide into groups of four people each. Each group form a circle and number yourselves from "1" to "4."

One person in a group will perform a movement, such as a jump or a knee-slap. The next person will repeat the movement, and add a different one, such as clapping overhead. The others in the group will continue the idea, each adding a movement, so that the last person is performing all the movements in order.

The next time around, a different person will begin. After four games, each person in each circle will have had a chance to start and to finish a game.

Try to think of other interesting movements.

The game may be extended in the following ways:

• Make a dance from the movements developed by your group. Think of ways to use repetition and variation in your dance.

• Add a drum accompaniment. Play it with a very slow, steady beat, one beat per movement.

Repeat a single movement within one drum beat.

Each person should continue his or her new movement after it is passed on to the next person.

• Change the direction of your movement. Remember that your dance needs some repetition to hold it together. It needs some variation to make it interesting.

• Add an accompaniment using other percussion instruments.

THE POLKA PATTERN

There are many ways of dancing to the song "Come and Dance," p. 124. For example, try the dance for "Weggis Song" with it, pp. 171–173. The step used for the Weggis dance is called a "heel-and-toe polka." Review the Weggis dance and then try it with "Come and Dance." You will need to repeat the steps for measures 1–8, and to begin the refrain with the steps for measure 9.

The basic polka step is as follows:

Step forward on the left foot. Bring the right toe to the left heel and transfer weight to right foot. Step again on the left foot, and hop. (This small "hop" is really the beginning of the next polka step.)

$\frac{2}{4}$ Count: <u>1</u> <u>and</u> <u>2</u> <u>and</u>
           step close step hop

Form a large circle. Move counter-clockwise as you practice the polka step to the music of "Come and Dance." Polka music is fast so your steps should be small and bouncy.

Now make a double circle of partners with boys on the inside. Partners join inside hands and stand side by side. Everyone moves counter-clockwise. Do polka steps moving forward in the circle with your partner.

When you can do this well, try a turning polka step. Do this by moving to the left around your partner. The boy will do the step in place, while the girl takes longer steps.

If you can do the steps listed above, you may wish to try a face-to-face, back-to-back polka. Use the same double-partner formation, with hands joined. This time, however, start with your outside foot (boy's left, girl's right). Do the first polka step turning toward each other while moving forward. Then swing hands forward and do a second step back-to-back, starting with the inside foot. Continue this pattern—face-to-face and back-to-back.

You may want to learn other ways of using this step.

Have fun with the polka!

GLOSSARY OF TERMS

accidentals—sharps, flats, or naturals that are not in the key signature, **87**

altered tones—tones raised or lowered a half step, **154**

arco—the playing of a stringed instrument by bowing, **40**

aria—a solo vocal piece with instrumental accompaniment, as in an opera or oratorio, **24**

articulation—the way the tones are begun and ended, **110**

augmentation—lengthening the note value of a theme or melody, **161**

ballerina—a female ballet dancer, **177**

baritone—low adult male voice with a range that lies between the tenor and bass voices, **19**

bass—the lowest male voice, **19**

blues—a style of jazz developed from Afro-American folk songs usually having a slow tempo and a sad subject, **211**

cadence—the ending of a phrase or section of music, **130**

calypso—improvised song, originally from the British West Indies, usually dealing with topical or humorous themes, **77**

celesta—a keyboard percussion instrument in which the hammers strike metal bars, **32**

changed voices—in girls and boys the voice undergoes a change between the ages of about twelve and sixteen; boys' voices may become lower, and girls' voices may become fuller in sound, **18**

chord root—the tone upon which a chord is built, **97**

choreographer—a person who plans the movements of dancers in a ballet, **177**

coda—additional music played or sung as an ending to a composition, **138**

concerto—a work for a solo instrument or group of solo instruments and orchestra, **233**

contralto—the lowest female voice, **18**

cut time—$\frac{2}{2}$ meter, often represented by the symbol ¢. —a direction to perform $\frac{4}{4}$ music briskly and treat the half note rather than the quarter note as the unit of time, **65**

descant—a countermelody, **20**

double stop—two tones played at the same time on a stringed instrument, **40**

duration—the length of time a musical sound exists, **62**

dynamics—degree of loudness or softness of a voice or instrument, **13**

expressive controls—tempo, dynamics, and articulation, **105**

fifth—an interval of five pitches between two tones, **102**

flat—a symbol (♭) indicating that a tone is to be lowered by a half step, **87**

fourth—an interval of four pitches between two tones, **102**

full cadence—a cadence that seems finished, **130**

gamelan—a Balinese orchestra, **144**

glissando—a sliding sound; on a violin it is made by sliding a finger along a string, **40**

harmonics—in a stringed instrument, the thin, silvery sound resulting from a light touching of a string, **40**

harmony—the sounding of 2 or more tones at the same time, **95**

harpsichord—a keyboard instrument, the strings of which are plucked, **231**

interval—the distance in pitch between two tones, **85**

irregular meter—a measure with an uneven number of beats, **80**

legato—tones that are smooth and connected, **42**

librettist—the person who writes the text of an opera or other long vocal composition, **182**

libretto—the text of an opera or other long vocal composition, **112, 182**

major scale—the arrangement of whole tones and half tones in the following pattern: w w $\frac{1}{2}$ w w w $\frac{1}{2}$, **88**

meter—the grouping of beats and accents within a measure, as shown by the time signature at the beginning of a musical composition, **65**

metronome—a mechanical device that is used to indicate exact tempo, **106**

mezzo-soprano—a woman's voice that lies between soprano and alto in range, **18**

minor scale—the arrangement of whole tones and half tones in the following pattern: w $\frac{1}{2}$ w w $\frac{1}{2}$ w w, **90**

movement—a main division of a long piece of music such as a symphony, **142**

natural sign—a symbol (♮) which cancels a sharp or a flat, **87**

pick-up note—a note or notes at the beginning of a musical composition, occurring immediately before the downbeat, **65**

octave displacement—the moving of some pitches of a melody into different octaves, **154**

opera—a drama told through acting, singing, and instrumental music, **182**

oratorio—a composition for solo voices, chorus, and orchestra, usually on a religious topic, **24**

ornamentation—the adding of notes to a melody for variation, **154**

ostinato—a repeated pattern, **138**

overture—music written as an introduction to an opera, an oratorio, a musical play, a ballet, or a suite, **48**

parallel thirds—harmony played at an interval of a third above or below a melody, **100**

pentatonic scale—a five-tone scale, **146**

percussionist—a performer on a percussion instrument, **28**

pizzicato—the playing of a stringed instrument by plucking, **40**

quartet—a four-member group, **36**

quintet—a five-member group, **30**

range—the extent (high-low) of the pitches within which a voice or instrument can sound, **13**

rhythm—the result of a grouping together of sounds having various durations, **62**

roll—the result of a fast repeated striking of a percussion instrument, **33**

second—an interval of two pitches between two tones, **102**

sequence—the repetition of a pattern or phrase at a different pitch, **150**

sharp—a symbol (♯) indicating that a note is to be raised by a half step, **87**

soprano—the highest female voice, **18**

staccato—tones that are short and separated, **42**

synthesizer a musical instrument through which any pitch can be produced electronically, **54**

tempo—the pace at which a piece of music is performed, **106**

tenor—the highest male voice, **105**

theme and variations—a musical form based on a theme in any number of variations, **167**

third—an interval of three pitches between two tones, **102**

timbre—the individual tone quality of any voice or instrument, **2**

triad—a chord of three tones consisting of the root and a third and a fifth above the root, **97**

trill—the rapid alternation of two tones, **33**

unchanged voice—the voice of a young girl or boy, **18**

uneven rhythm—the result of music with dotted patterns, **70**

variation—a modification or altered version of a given musical passage, **149**

variation form—same as *theme and variations,* **167**

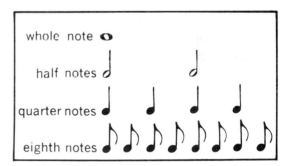

CLASSIFIED INDEX

Animals, Birds
Bumblebees Sip Honey
(listening), **145**
Camptown Races, **99, 312**
Cuckoo, **301**
Go Tell Aunt Rhody, **98**
I Ride an Old Paint, **156**
Mi Caballo Blanco, **63**
Morning Song, **107**
My Home's in Montana, **152**
Never Argue with a Bee, **87, 309**
Oh, Willow, **114**
Painted Bird, The, **133**
Papageno's Song, **240**
Rain, **91**
Two Cats (painting), **66**
Winter Now Is Over, The, **20**

Careers
Orchestrator, **110**
Organist, **167**
Radio Announcer, **233**
Violinist, Cellist, **40**

Folk Songs
Afro-American
Aardvarks on the Ark, **289**
I'm Gonna Sing, **8**
I'm on My Way, **122**
Nobody Knows the Trouble I've
Seen, **85**
When the Saints Go Marching In,
162

America (see also Afro-American)
Black Is the Color, **23**
Buffalo Gals, **150**

Camptown Races, **99, 312**
Chicka-Hanka, **140**
Come, Come, Ye Saints, **216**
Down in the Valley, **299**
Go Tell Aunt Rhody, **98**
Hey Ho! Anybody Home?, **139**
I Ride an Old Paint, **156**
Johnny Morgan, **34**
Long Gone, **74**
Man Who Has Plenty of Good
Peanuts, The, **89**
My Home's in Montana, **152, 310**
Old Joe Clark, **174, 311**
Old Dan Tucker, **214**
Pat Works on the Railway, **127**
Singing School, The, **218**
Sourwood Mountain, **121**
Streets of Laredo, The, **300**
When Johnny Comes Marching
Home, **160**

Austria
Cuckoo, **301**
Haidschi Bumbaidschi, **100**

Canada
Voyageur's Song, **220**

Chile
Mi Caballo Blanco, **63**
Tortilla Man, The, **12**

Czechoslovakia
Come and Dance, **124**

England, Scotland, Wales
Ash Grove, The, **44**
Let Simon's Beard Alone, **222**
May Day Carol, The, **267**

Tomorrow Is St. Valentine's Day,
265
Washing Day, **131**
Wraggle Taggle Gypsies, The, **223**

France
Auprès de Ma Blonde, **136**
March of the Three Kings, **48**

Jamaica
Watah Come a Me Eye, **280**

Germany
Holla Hi, Holla Ho, **306**
Vigolin, **38**

Ireland
Cockles and Mussels, **26**

Israel
Let Us Sing and Rejoice, **92**
Shalom Chaverim, **90**

Italy-Switzerland
Tiritomba (Italian), **128**
Winter Now Is Over, The
(Italo-Swiss), **20**

Latin-America
Painted Bird, The, **133**

Mexico
Christmas Carol, **41**
Morning Song, **107**
Quién les da Posada, **256**

Norway
On the Hillside, **264**

Poland
Infant Jesus, King of Glory, **262**

Puerto Rico
La Calle Ancha, **123**

Russia
Down the Peterskaya Road, **178**

Spain
At the Gate of Heaven, **134**
Tambourine, The, **159**

Switzerland
Weggis Song, **172**

Trinidad
Mary Ann, **76, 313**

Yugoslavia
Stoyan's Wife, **81**

Foreign Languages
French
Auprès de Ma Blonde, **136**
March of the Three Kings, **48**

German
Haidschi Bumbaidschi, **100**

Hebrew
Shalom Chaverim, **90**

Spanish
At the Gate of Heaven, **134**
Christmas Carol, **41**
La Calle Ancha, **123**
Mi Caballo Blanco, **63**
Morning Song, **107**
Painted Bird, The, **133**
Quién les da Posada, **256**
Tortilla Man, The, **12**

Freedom Songs
Come, Come, Ye Saints, **216**
Revolutionary Tea, **224**
Star-Spangled Banner, The, **270**

Holidays, Special Days

Chanukah Is Here, **250**

Christmas Carol, **41**

Christmas Greeting, A, **252**

Halloween, **245**

Hark! The Herald Angels Sing, **260**

Holly and the Ivy, The, **253**

Infant Jesus, King of Glory, **262**

Joy to the World, **258**

March of the Three Kings, **48**

May Day Carol, The, **267**

Morning Song (Birthdays), **107**

Praise, O Praise!
   (Thanksgiving), **249**

Quién les da Posada, **256**

Thanksgiving Song, **248**

This Is My Country, **3**

Tomorrow Is St. Valentine's Day,
   265

Twelve Days of Christmas, The, **254**

You're a Grand Old Flag, **278**

Patriotic Songs

America, **165**

Battle Hymn of the Republic, **68**

Star-Spangled Banner, The, **270**

Texas, Our Texas, **287**

Poetry

American Heritage, **275**

Christmas Is Remembering, **252**

Electric Room, The, **59**

I Hear America Singing, **164**

Life Styles: Two Variations, **168**

Moonlight, **104**

My Native Land, **269**

Open Range, **151**

Remember September, **243**

Springtime Is a Green Time, **241**

Welcome to the New Year, **263**

Your Own Dance, **176**

Popular

Baroquin' Rock, **228**

Changing, **205**

It's a Small World, **208**

Man Must Be Free, **82**

Rounds, Canons

Christmas Greeting, A, **252**

Crossroads of America, **14**

Evening, **96**

Hey, Ho! Anybody Home?, **139**

It's Such a Joy, **284**

Let Simon's Beard Alone, **222**

Morning, **66, 96**

Shalom Chaverim, **90**

Singing School, The, **218**

Seasonal and Environmental

America, **165**

Auprès de Ma Blonde, **136**

Ash Grove, The, **44**

Church Bells Ringing, Rainy
   Winter Night (painting), **91**

Cuckoo, **301**

Farewell to Thee, **304**

Flowers That Bloom in the Spring,
   116

Hawaiian Surf, **302**

Lullaby, **94**

May Day Carol, The, **267**

My Home's in Montana, **152**

Night Mist, **109**

On the Hillside, **264**

Papageno's Song, **240**

Sing Your Way Home, **10**

Swinging Along, **242**

Tiritomba, **128**

Voyageur's Song, **220**

Weggis Song, **172**

Wide Fields, The, **4**

Winter Now Is Over, The, **20**

Song Stories, Opera, Plays, Ballet

Amahl and the Night Visitors,
   182-201

Mikado, The, **112-117**

Petrouchka, **179-181**

Songs with Ostinatos

Chicka-Hanka, **140**

Hey, Ho! Anybody Home?, **139**

Making Music with Ostinatos, **146**

Work Songs

Chicka-Hanka, **140**

Cockles and Mussels, **26**

Drill, Ye Tarriers, **64**

I Ride an Old Paint, **156**

Long Gone, **74**

My Home's in Montana, **152**

Pat Works on the Railway, **127**

Tired Cowboy, A, **285**

Washing Day, **131**

LISTENING SELECTIONS

Afro-Chinese Minuet
(*H. Partch*), **155**

American Salute
(*M. Gould*), **161**

Baby Elephant Walk
(*H. Mancini*), **72**

Bizet Has His Day
(*L. Brown*), **211**

Bumblebees Sip Honey
(Balinese Dance Music), **145**

Cattle from THE PLOW THAT
BROKE THE PLAINS
(*V. Thomson*), **157**

Choros No. 6-bis for Violin and
Cello (*H. Villa-Lobos*), **40**

Clair de Lune,
Arranged for Orchestra
(*C. Debussy*), **105**

Concerto for Orchestra, Second
Movement
(*B. Bartók*), **102**

CONCERTO IN G MAJOR FOR
VIOLIN AND ORCHESTRA,
First Movement
(*A. Vivaldi*), **233**

Dance of the Sugarplum Fairy
from THE NUTCRACKER SUITE
(*P. Tchaikovsky*), **32**

Fantasy on a Mexican
Christmas Carol
(*R. McBride*), **42**

Farandole from L'ARLÉSIENNE
SUITE NO. 2
(*G. Bizet*), **47**

Geographical Fugue
(*E. Toch*), **16**

Greeting Prelude
(*I. Stravinsky*), **155**

Happiness from *You're a Good
Man, Charlie Brown*
(*C. Gesner*), **207**

He Shall Feed His Flock from
THE MESSIAH
(*G. Handel*), **24**

Improvisation for Solo
Performers and 5 Tape Recorders
(*G. Polski*), **55**

Minuet II From FRENCH SUITE NO.1
IN D MINOR, Rock Arrangement
(*J.S. Bach*), **230**

Navy Hymn
(Arr. for Orchestra), **275**

OCTOBER MOUNTAIN, Second
and Fourth Movements
(X. Hovhaness), **29**

Ostinatos from TABUH-
TABUHAN
(C. McPhee), **145**

Oven Grill Concerto
(A. Biasini and L. Pogonowski), **58**

Overture (excerpt) from
L'ARLÉSIENNE SUITE NO. 1
(G. Bizet), **47**

PETROUCHKA, excerpts
(I. Stravinsky), **179**

Piece 4 from FIVE PIECES FOR
ORCHESTRA, Op. 10
(A. Webern), **52**

QUARTET IN C MAJOR, Op. 33,
No. 3 ("The Bird"), Fourth Movement
(F. Haydn), **236**

St. Louis Blues
(W.C. Handy), **211**

Sketch for Percussion
(R. Lo Presti), **33**

Sonata, Allegro, March, and
Battle from BATTALIA
(I. Biber), **232**

Souvenir de Porto Rico
(L.M. Gottschalk), **78**

STRING QUARTET NO. 4,
Movement 2 *(H. Cowell)*, **142**

Syncopated Clock
(L. Anderson), **110**

Variations on "America"
(C. Ives), **167**

ALPHABETICAL SONG INDEX

Aardvarks on the Ark, **289**

Aloha Oe (Farewell to Thee), **304**

Alphabet, The, **111**

Amahl and the Night Visitors, **183**

America, **165**

Are You Sleeping?, **298**

Ash Grove, The, **44**

At the Gate of Heaven, **134**

Auprès de Ma Blonde, **136**

Baroquin' Rock, **228**

Battle Hymn of the Republic, **68**

Behold the Lord High Executioner, **113**

Black Is the Color, **23**

Buffalo Gals, **150**

Camptown Races, **99, 312**

Changing, **205**

Chanukah Is Here, **250**

Chicka-Hanka, **140**

Christmas Carol, **41**

Christmas Greeting, A, **252**

Cockles and Mussels, **26**

Come and Dance, **124**

Come, Come, Ye Saints, **216**

Crossroads of America, **14**

Cuckoo, **301**

Down in the Valley, **299**

Down the Peterskaya Road, **178**

Drill, Ye Tarriers, **64**

Eternal Father, Strong to Save, **274**

Evening, **96**

Farewell to Thee (Aloha Oe), **304**

Flowers That Bloom in the Spring,
The, **116**

Good Luck, **234**

Go Tell Aunt Rhody, **98**

Haidschi, Bumbaidschi, **100**

Hallowe'en, **245**

Hark! The Heralds Angels Sing, **260**

Hawaiian Surf, **302**

Heavens Resound, The, **238**

Hey, Ho! Anybody Home?, **139**

Holla Hi, Holla Ho, **306**

Holly and the Ivy, The, **253**

How Good It Is to Sing Together, **283**

I'm Gonna Sing, **8**

I'm on My Way, **122**

Infant Jesus, King of Glory, **262**

Instruments, The, **50**

I Ride an Old Paint, **156**

It's a Small World, **208**

It's Such a Joy, **284**

Johnny Morgan, **34**

Joy to the World, **258**

La Calle Ancha, **123**

Let Simon's Beard Alone, **222**

Let There Be Peace on Earth, **272**

Let Us Sing and Rejoice, **92**

Long Gone, **74**

Lullaby, **94**

Mahalo Nui, **307**

Man Must Be Free, **82**

Man Who Has Plenty of Good Peanuts, The, **89**

March of the Three Kings, **48**

Mary Ann, **76, 313**

May Day Carol, The, **267**

Mi Caballo Blanco, **63**

Morning, **66, 96**

Morning Song, **107**

My Home's in Montana, **152, 310**

Never Argue with a Bee, **87, 309**

Night Mist, **109**

Nobody Knows the Trouble I've Seen, **85**

Oh-Willow, **114**

Old Dan Tucker, **214**

Old Joe Clark, **174, 311**

On the Hillside, **264**

Painted Bird, The, **133**

Papageno's Song, **240**

Pat Works on the Railway, **127**

Praise, O Praise, **249**

Quién les da Posada, **256**

Rain, **91**

Revolutionary Tea, **224**

Shalom Chaverim, **90**

Singing School, The, **218**

Sing Your Way Home, **10**

Sourwood Mountain, **121**

Star-Spangled Banner, The, **270**

Stoyan's Wife, **81**

Streets of Laredo, The, **300**

Swinging Along, **242**

Tambourine, The, **159**

Texas, Our Texas, **287**

Thanksgiving Song, **248**

This Is My Country, **3**

Tired Cowboy, A, **285**

Tiritomba, **128**

Tomorrow Is St. Valentine's Day, **265**

Tortilla Man, The, **12**

Twelve Days of Christmas, The, **254**

Vigolin, **38**

Voyageur's Song, **220**

Washing Day, **131**

Watah Come a Me Eye, **280**

Weggis Song, **172**

When Johnny Comes Marching Home, **160**

When the Saints Go Marching In, **162**

Wide Fields, The, **4**

Winter Now Is Over, The, **20**

Wraggle Taggle Gypsies, The, **223**

You're a Grand Old Flag, **278**

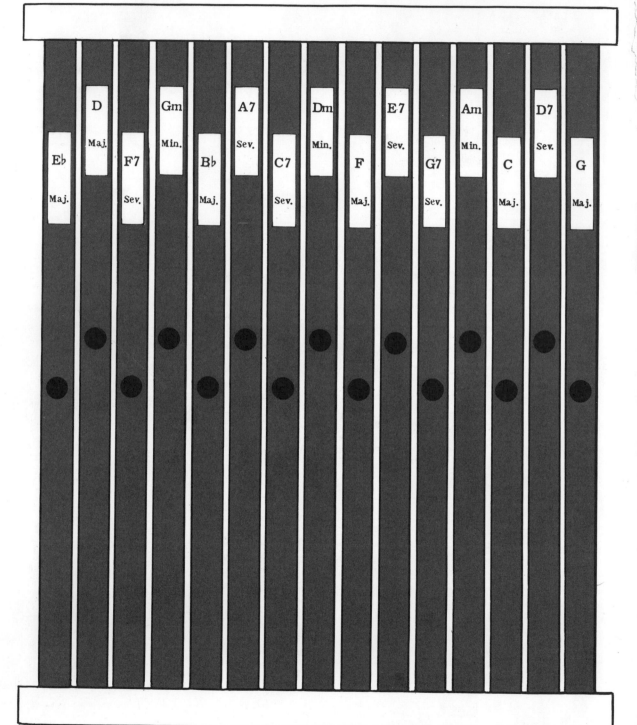